EXPECT

Trusting God t...

Melvin Banks

Marshall Pickering
An Imprint of HarperCollinsPublishers

Marshall Pickering is an Imprint of
HarperCollins*Religious*
Part of HarperCollins*Publishers*
77–85 Fulham Palace Road, London W6 8JB

First published in Great Britain
in 1995 by Marshall Pickering

1   3   5   7   9   10   8   6   4   2

A catalogue record for this book is
available from the British Library

0551 02924-2

Printed and bound in Great Britain by
HarperCollins*Manufacturing* Glasgow

CONTENTS

MIRACLES IN THE FALKLANDS

I was prayerfully thumbing through the huge pile of letters in my hands. I had been away some weeks, and the mail had accumulated in the office, but as usual I wanted to see every letter. As I prayed over the request of a mum for a dying eight year-old, I noted tearstains on the edge of the letter. In another letter a doctor asked for prayer for an incurable disease that had seized him. He wanted to travel 200 miles to receive the laying on of hands at one of my healing services. There were many others. My staff and I try to answer all the letters personally, and we pray over each need or request.

As she passed by my wife Lilian told me, 'By the way, someone wants you to preach in the Falklands!' I looked up, smiled at her joke, and went praying over another letter.

'Have a look in that pile there,' she added, in all seriousness. I reached across the office desk, thumbed through the pile, and there was a handwritten note from an 80-year-old lady:

I've been praying for the islands all my life, my mother before me . . . but no revival, people are stiff-necked, hard-hearted. I would love to see revival in my lifetime. I don't think I've got all that much time left. God will use you, if you come. Things are getting worse here spiritually, folk are getting further and further away from God. Please come to the Falklands – give them a chance!

The letter caused a vibration in my spirit, a heart rending, yet a strong feeling of assurance that there was hope for these folk. I began looking at maps of the Falklands and researching the islands' history, culture, and religion. I began to make it a focus of my prayers. Should I go to the Falklands? It was a long way to go – an 18-hour journey by RAF jet over 8,000 miles of ocean, all for 2,000 people scattered over two remote islands with no roads or transport. Should I spend a week preaching to them, when in our big English cities there are millions who need to hear the gospel?

GOD SPOKE

But my mind went back to some 18 months previously, when I was in deep prayer in the summer hut at the end of the garden at my home in Wiltshire. Then God had spoken to me with fresh clarity: 'I will send you where my Word has not been heard. I will send you to people who have not received the evangel. I will send you across the sea. I will send you to the ends of the earth with my power and message.'

I had already preached in 35 nations, so what did God mean by 'where my Word has not been heard'? I did not know it then, but God meant that he was going to send me to the Falklands, to Republican areas of Northern Ireland, to the Muslims and Hindus in the UK. You will read about all this in later chapters. Now the first part of God's word to me was about to be executed: the Falklands revival was about to begin.

Through this revival I was to cultivate a new closeness to my Saviour, he was to humble me as never before, God was going to put a hook in my jaw and draw me to the foot of his cross, making me totally reliant on him. Once again I was to see the Living God bring us into the realm of his supernatural power.

I found that the churches in the Falklands, like many in the UK, were struggling. Their membership was very low. Most were orthodox in doctrine and well run; some had beautiful ritual or eloquent preaching; but they all lacked a blazing, burning love for Christ. They were weary of trying to persuade people to believe the gospel. But God was about to shower them with untold power.

For years they had been diligently sowing, and they were about to reap the harvest. 'We saw the splendour and grandeur of God return,' one islander wrote to me later. 'We gazed on him, we saw his reserves of power, we were enhanced in His presence.'

When revival comes, as it did in the Falklands, it shakes, it is disturbing, it is unexpected, it is different and not according to our plans!

I boarded an RAF Tristar at Brize Norton in Oxfordshire. There is no commercial air service to the Falklands: all flights are military and carry only a few civilians.

GRILLED

Before boarding I had been grilled by some security officers. Since the war back in 1982 all visitors to the islands have had to be carefully checked. They could not understand why the Falklands needed a 'Billy Graham type evangelist', but after some queries, I finally made it through on to the plane.

As I sat on the plane, surrounded by soldiers, they

gazed at me, a civilian, with some curiosity, wondering why I was going to such an out-of-the-way place. I had flown a hundred times before, preaching in nations all over the world, and yet on this flight I felt strangely nervous. I am often nervous on the first night of a mission, especially when TV, radio or press reporters are present. Above all I feel nervous when a great crowd of sick people look to me to bring them deliverance through our wonderful Lord Jesus Christ.

Yet here I was nervous even before I had arrived in the Falklands. The devil seemed to whisper, 'You are mad spending thousands of pounds of God's money on this venture. All this time going 8,000 miles to the ends of the earth for one old lady! No one will come. You will be preaching to one or two people. It will be a wasted journey, wasted finances . . .' So the thoughts crowded in.

Then I turned to God's Word. Opening my small New Testament, my eyes fell on Revelation chapter 3: 'I know your works.' God was saying that he had planned it all: he knew what was best for me. Then it went on, and I nearly leapt through the roof of the jet: 'If God opens the door, no man can close it; if God closes the door, no man can open it.' Soon after that I fell asleep, at complete peace!

The journey was long but uneventful, punctuated only by a brief stop at Ascension Island. My first view of the Falklands was San Carlos Bay, famous for the Welsh Guards' historic landing. Then we flew over the bare, rugged hills and plains. I saw iced-over lakes, small rivers and even some steamer ducks in flight, their black-tipped wings clearly visible from the plane window. Finally we touched down at the big military base at Mount Pleasant.

As we taxied across the tarmac, I could see many Army personnel. They were wrapped up warmly, trying to protect themselves from the sharp, cutting wind (it was mid-winter here in the Falklands). Little did I know that God's warming fire from heaven was about to break out with blessing on hundreds of lives.

We presented ourselves at the small terminus, and an Army sergeant with a loud voice warned us about the many live minefields which remained on the Islands, showing us exact replicas of mines. After this I moved through 'civvy' customs, where an older official whispered to me, 'You are more than welcome' with a warm smile. I later learned that he went to my meetings and found the joy of a new dedication to Christ in his life.

Then I went out into the bitter cold, where someone was waiting to pick me up. The 34-mile journey by Land Rover took an hour and a half, and was very rough. I hit the top of the vehicle a few times! We were on the only main road in the Falklands, which leads from the Mount Pleasant base to Port Stanley. The road was built only a few years ago; it is stony and not tarred, except for the final few hundred metres.

We passed Fitzroy and the edge of Bluff Cove, then in the mist above us I saw Mount Tumbledown, which I thought was an awesome sight – a rugged terrain rising up into this magnificent mount. It looked so strong, staring down on Stanley Harbour, barren yet beautiful, snow-capped like a glistening jewel in the distance.

My first view of Port Stanley was of the tin roofs, the little bungalows and the concrete roads. The only cars I saw were Land Rovers. Some of the homes were made of wood and corrugated iron, while others were made from hardy stone out of the hills. We drove down the main street, which was muddy with so many Land Rovers from the hills scurrying back and forth. I noted radio aerials on every vehicle. There is little TV in the Isles, so the people listen to their radios all day long.

My first impression was how tiny the town was, with its small, quaint houses, many of them painted white, and its rough pavements. Everything was clean and English-looking; it was almost a pioneer community.

I was dropped off at the main 'hotel', a small guesthouse on Port Stanley Waterside. It was empty when I arrived. The staff welcomed me warmly, but they thought I was an oddity! Evangelists were almost unknown in the Falklands.

After a cup of tea, I refused a hearty meal, remembering an old Pentecostal preacher's advice to me years before: 'Much eating – poor meeting!' Instead I gave myself to earnest prayer. There seemed to be a calm and quietness before the storm. I felt lonely, but I knew the Lord was with me. He seemed to say, 'Stand still and see the salvation of your God.'

BETTY MILLER

Eventually it was time to get ready for the first meeting. After getting some directions from the hotelier, I went to meet Mrs Betty Miller, the sprightly 80-year-old who had written to me for nearly two years, asking for videos, tapes, books and prayers. She had invited me to come to the Isles. At first I had been reluctant to go. I had thought that there would be little interest. It was so far to go for a few people, and the financial cost was great. But she had pleaded, prayed and begged for me to come. She wanted to see a revival in the Falklands before she died. She had been praying for it for 75 years! She had given much of her inheritance to sponsor the visit, and others had also given small sums to help.

Through the dimly lit streets I made my way. There was hardly anyone about. I could see lights in the houses; everyone seemed to be keeping themselves warm in their tiny homes. I wondered if anyone would come to the meetings at all.

I knocked nervously on the door of 1 St John's Street. A voice within said, 'Come in.' I opened the door – people in the Falklands leave their doors unlocked! The hallway light went on, and there stood the tall, thin figure of Betty.

'I'm Melvin Banks,' I said.

She smiled, gave a whoop and declared, 'The day of the Lord has come for the Falklands!' She warmly shook my hand.

Soon we were sitting in her little 1940s-style kitchen enjoying a cup of tea. Together we prayed, talked and planned.

'We will put out 30 or 40 chairs. If they are filled, that will be a miracle!' she declared.

I walked out into the night towards the school hall. The lights had already been put on by the caretaker. A couple of beautiful storm petrels darted across the wind in front of me. As I entered the hall I noted the Falklands coat of arms and motto on a wall: *Desire the right*. What a great theme to start with!

DEPENDING ON GOD

The mission was not officially supported by the churches of the islands. In any case, they had very few members. I had no one to rely on but Betty, and the two other Christians who had given her some help with sending a letter to every house and farm and family in the Isles, with an invitation to the crusade. We were depending on God.

I sat there waiting. Two ladies had turned up by 7.20 p.m. There were only ten minutes to go – would anyone else come? My faith almost wilted. 'You left people queueing up in the street to get in to your last crusade,' I reflected. 'In Coventry two weeks ago 1,000 people were converted. A few weeks ago you had to call the police out in Scunthorpe to control the crowds trying to get in. Here you are with four people including Betty and yourself, with nine minutes to go, and the streets as quiet as a ghost-town!'

Then with a noise almost as loud as that made by the Royal Marines' entry into Port Stanley eleven years before, the doors flew open and a crowd rushed through! Soon we were running everywhere to get more chairs, and almost 50 had turned up. They were quiet, and they slowly learnt the hymns and worship songs. I gave an evangelistic message.

During the meeting the Canon of the Cathedral quietly crept on to the back row. He was cautious, but during the week his attitude changed as his wife's cancerous lump vanished from her body through prayer to Christ.

In particular they liked the chorus, 'All over the world the Spirit is moving' – it was very applicable there, at the bottom of the globe! They sang with gusto – fishing folk, hardy shepherds, country people, farmers and whalers. Many of them wore the chunky Falklands pullover; most of the women wore trousers, even in the meetings.

At the very first meeting 18 people were converted

and I prayed for the sick. Many were curious, for it was all entirely new to them. Most of the people who came were not churchgoers.

The first person I laid hands on was a lady with crippling, painful arthritis. Her name was Eileen. I didn't know it then, but she was famous on the Isles. She was not a Christian, but she was a woman of very good character who was known and liked by everyone. She had been awarded an OBE by the Queen at Buckingham Palace. She was instantly healed. She was able to move every limb and bone. All the pain vanished. Since she was so well known, her healing encouraged many others with sicknesses to seek God's healing touch. What a confirmation that God really had wanted me to go to the Falklands – that the first person I prayed for was someone whom everyone would know and believe!

The next day the local BBC radio station became interested. They carried Eileen's remarkable testimony four times, for 20 minutes each time, after the weather forecasts. The whole community had heard of the miracle within 24 hours!

After that people flocked to the meetings by plane, Land Rover, on horseback and on foot. The hall was packed out the next night. The Canon, encouraged by his wife's healing, turned up and begged to help. What a blessing he became to me! We became very close friends. That night I sent people away with the Word ringing in their ears. Many more were converted and healed.

In the days that followed I preached the Word day and night. The response from the people was so strong that we held some extra meetings. Great healings became the talk everywhere. It opened the people's hearts and led nearly 200 to salvation.

Some folk who had been almost blind were healed so powerfully that they could read the smallest print without glasses. One person who had been profoundly deaf had to move his clock out of his bedroom, because after he had been healed the ticking was too loud for him!

I realized that God had immersed me in a revival. I was not worthy of being used in this way. Without him I would have been stranded; it was the Holy Spirit who energized me. Those who were spiritually starving to death after years of empty religion were being set free!

Soon people were inviting friends and relatives in isolated parts of the islands to come and not miss the revival. The entire community was being moved and shaken by the Holy Ghost.

MEETING THE GOVERNOR

Soon I was called to Royal Government House to meet the Governor, his excellency William A. Fullerton, CMG. He was not a believer, and usually spent his Sundays on his yacht. He told his secretary, 'I'll give Mr Banks about five minutes.' His secretary whispered back, 'Don't make it more – we have those important oil men afterwards.'

We sat down in the room where in 1982 the Argentine commander had signed the surrender document, after the seizure of Government House by the British Paras in a bloody battle. Tea and cakes were brought in on a nice silver platter. We talked of the healing power of God. Mr Fullerton seemed very interested and asked many questions. Some friends of his had been healed. Everyone was talking about what God was doing. Each time the secretary popped his head round the door, the Governor said, 'Five minutes more'!

This incident reminded me of the apostle Paul's interview with King Agrippa in Acts 25. Agrippa too was fascinated by the power of God. I told Mr Fullerton about the Saviour and healer of all men, Jesus Christ, who is the same today as he was in apostolic times. We prayed together and he thanked me for seeing him.

Soon it was spreading like wild-fire, as people with long-term diseases were instantly and completely cured by God's grace and mercy. I was soon called out to pray for bed-ridden and housebound people. I was kept so busy that I was getting exhausted.

John was a well-known painter and craftsman. He had been unable to make anything or to play his beloved organ for some years, due to crippled hands. He looked a pitiful sight; it took him some time to get to the door. I led him to Christ in his home. Then I prayed and God wonderfully healed him. He then came to the meetings and played his organ for us – *God changed that man*. He walked around town doing things he had not done for years.

Radio carried the stories of miracles daily. The crowds packed the school hall to capacity. I had to leave after a week, since my flight was already booked. But the Christians prayed that the weather would keep me there, so they could have more meetings. But I had a tight schedule in the UK, so I prayed that the flight would be on time. But on the day I was due to go home the plane met such bad weather that it had to turn back to Ascension Island. Their prayers in that direction were stronger than mine!

We held further meetings. These became so packed that the Canon asked us to come to the Cathedral. A great crowd turned up. Many came to the altar as I asked sinners to repent and come forward. Such a thing had never been seen before in Christ Church Cathedral!

Eventually the weather improved and my plane landed. With tears in my eyes I said 'goodbye' to my friends. The work was to go on and the revival continued. In the months afterwards the local press gave whole pages to people who were still radiant, saved and cured of their diseases. It was a great witness to the power of Christ.

The Canon was promoted, being made Canon in charge of the Royal Chapel, in the Tower of London, and Domestic Chaplain to the Queen. I have been invited to visit the Royal Chapel and share with them there, possibly the first Pentecostal to do so.

The incidents of healing have continued. The years of prayer by Betty Miller and her mother have been answered. God heard the faithful prayers of two Christian ladies and sent a revival.

I nearly didn't go to the Falklands – I nearly missed this arresting, glorious visitation of God. I'm glad I listened to the Lord. I'm glad he took away my pride and made me willing to go 8,000 miles because of one old lady's persistence. The result was miracle after miracle, as the islands were touched by the gospel message that Christ is alive and real today. Never say 'no' to Jesus. Be obedient to him, be open, always willing. Say 'yes' and keep saying 'yes' – that's the way to victory and revival. Surrender, surrender, surrender – that's the message behind the Falklands miracle.

2

REVIVAL IN PARAMILITARY COUNTRY

I was about to leave for some meetings in Ireland. It was late at night and I had to rise early to get to my plane from Bristol airport the following morning. The phone rang. It was my good friend George Hamnet of Clevedon. He often chauffeurs me around to crusades if I am too exhausted to drive through heavy traffic.

'Hello, Melvin,' he said. 'I've got a scripture for you.'

I could hardly keep my eyes open, but I replied, 'Go on, George . . .'

'John chapter 6, verse 1 onwards.'

I noted it down.

'Praying for you, Melvin . . .' He hung up.

I staggered into bed after my customary prayers. Then before switching off the bedside lamp, I picked up my Bible and found John 6:1. These verses were to be a prophetic word about the revival which was about to break out in Ireland: 'Some time after this, Jesus crossed to the far shore of the Sea of Galilee . . . and a great crowd of people followed him because they saw the miraculous signs he had performed on the sick.' What a wonderful word to launch this Irish revival, which, in some areas, was the first for 400 years.

Just after this, on my arrival in Northern Ireland, I was to preach in the magnificent new Mountain Lodge Church at Darkley, County Armagh. It was a glorious, sunny Easter Sunday. The cars poured up narrow lanes to the new car park. Hundreds of people were coming to this, the first of the revival meetings. Alongside the great new structure sat the simple gospel hut which had formerly been the fellowship's meeting-place.

As I walked the aisles between the wooden benches I saw the plaque on the wall which was a memorial to that awful night seven years before when this Pentecostal church became a household name on the lips of millions around the world. The incident was called the 'slaughter of the innocents'.

GOSPEL HALL MASSACRE

Here on 20 November, as the evening service was commencing with the singing of the old gospel hymn, 'There is power, power, wonder-working power in the blood of the Lamb', three Republican terrorists with automatic weapons stepped into the little gospel hall, packed with 90 or so men, women and children and gunned them down. Ten people were killed, including three elders. Many others were maimed for life. One survivor had to have seven bullets removed from her body.

It was called the 'gospel hall massacre' by the world's press. The *Daily Mirror* called it 'Horror in a humble hut on the hill'. The bravery of the elders, Mr Wilson, Mr Brown and Mr Cunningham, in seeking to tackle the gunmen unarmed, was amazing. David Wilson, although shot and bleeding, ran into the hall shouting warnings for everyone to get down; he gave his life to save others. Pastor Bob Bain spoke the message of Christian forgiveness to the world's press, saying that he would forgive the killers and that the church would pray for them. Quoted in one national newspaper, Pastor Bain said, 'There can be no thoughts of revenge; these people must be saved.'

Nearly 900 letters came from all over the world, including one from Prime Minister Margaret Thatcher and one from the President of the Irish Republic. The Roman Catholic Bishop of Armagh visited the widows. The Spirit of God took charge of the situation as senior policemen, political leaders, doctors, nurses, priests, ministers, Protestants and Roman Catholics were moved to tears by the stoical spirit of these gracious, forgiving, loving, Holy Ghost filled believers. This massacre moved the world and brought the heart of the Christian faith to millions.

It so happened that a tape recording was being made of that service, and in the chaos no one thought to turn the machine off. The result was a shocking but very moving recording. On it one heard the church members singing praise to God, and then suddenly the firing of the guns, the cries, the screams . . . Many people were converted through this recording. The world learnt anew that the Pentecostal people were compassionate, determined, strong, solid, Bible-believing folk of the highest calibre. This terrible crime against such good, law-abiding people shook the world. Its spiritial impact was enormous.

The old building reopened for worship two months later. The national media carried it into millions of homes – 'Darkley survivors pray again' and 'Re-opening of massacre church – defiant Darkley', the headlines reported. Since then revival blessing has swept through the area. The church has opened two new branch churches. Scores were converted and healed during my short crusade there. The work booms and grows, its impact on the local community immense.

The completion of the big new church building on the mountain-top tells the whole world that God's people are crushed but not destroyed. We are not and cannot ever be disinherited. Nothing will deter us; 'No weapon forged against us can prosper'; we are 'more than conquerors through him that loved us'; he will 'withhold no good thing to them that fear him'; and 'nothing can separate us, neither life nor death nor any living thing, from the love of God our Saviour'.

I had been in prayer sometime prior to this. I was particularly seeking God, that he would not only give me revival and a greater harvest of souls than I had ever seen in my previous 30 years of ministry, but also that he would open doors for me to preach where he had never been proclaimed. God was about to answer my prayer and turn back 400 years of history as he did it.

The name 'IRA' kept coming to my mind in prayer. Knowing about these people through the TV and papers, I thought this idea in my mind was from the devil. But each day as I prayed, it kept coming to me: 'IRA . . . IRA . . .'

After one evening meeting at the Mountain Lodge Church I went out into the dark. God had given us many conversions and miracles of healing. It had been a wonderful night! I looked out into the night and saw the lights stretched out on a hillside some distance away. I asked the pastor the name of that area. He replied, 'That's the Republican area.' As he drove me back to my digs, I asked if they ever had meetings there. He replied, 'I've not been there for 20 years. It's very dangerous.'

BEYOND REDEMPTION?

Another pastor told me, 'They are beyond redemption!' Another told of one nationalist town where a gospel tent had been burnt down. Another said they had tried to have an open-air meeting, going up with a gospel van, when hooded gunmen came and gave them five minutes to vanish, or they would all be shot, menacing them with automatic rifles. But God was speaking to me.

I was in safe Protestant country, sitting in a farmhouse one morning, when there was a knock at the door. In came a visitor who asked the host if he could see me. He knew nothing of my enquiries and prayers about the Republican areas, or about the vision that had come to me. He pointed at me and said, 'The Protestants ought to be ashamed of themselves. They have had the Bible for hundreds of years and have done nothing with it! When will you give our people a chance to be saved?'

He was a converted Roman Catholic. He told me he had come to a personal knowledge of our Lord in a dramatic experience. Later he had spoken in tongues like the apostles had. Now he led a little group of about 20 Christians – all were from a notorious Republican estate and had found Jesus through his testimony. He begged me to come to his area. I pointed out that evangelists were usually threatened with violence in the Republican areas.

He said, 'They will not touch you. You have the key to victory. You have a powerful, miraculous gift of healing and miracles. It will conquer because it is Christ's gift to reach these people's hearts.' I was so touched by this appeal that I agreed to go to this town.

On the first night, unheralded except by a minimum of advertising, I stood in front of a vast crowd packed to the doors of the hall; many were standing. We could not sing our usual worship songs, as 99 per cent of the audience were quite unaccustomed to such a service.

There was a quiet, tense atmosphere. I stood and

made it clear to the wide-eyed, serious-looking people that I came simply with a message from God. I came with the blood of Christ and the Holy Spirit as my power and strength. Scores became converted following a simple 20-minute gospel talk.

The first person I prayed for was an elderly lady bent over with arthritis and creeping along on two sticks. She looked at me with a wrinkled face and blue Irish eyes, longing for some relief. I cast the devil out and commanded the disease to go. The people waited, hardly able to breathe, to see what would happen. God immediately released and perfectly healed her on the spot! She ran around and did a jig in the aisle – it brought the place down! I've not seen such excitement. They danced, jigged, clapped and praised God.

Then a big, tough-looking woman rushed out of her seat towards me. I wondered what was happening. I thought she was about to hit me as she raised her arm – but she brought it down around me in a great bear-hug! She gave me a big smacker of a kiss on my cheek and declared, 'That was my mother. She hasn't walked like that for ten years!'

One after another, for two hours, I prayed for hundreds. Little kiddies were handed back to their mothers well again. Empty wheelchairs piled up by the door and sticks against the wall.

HEAVEN CAME DOWN

The miracles of Christ won over the hearts of hundreds. Night after night the revival continued, with people queueing in the rain for hours to get in. We held many extra services and we had to tell the people they were not allowed to stay for more than one service per night, to make way for the second crowd already queueing around the block.

Out of a population of only 10,000, about 7,000 came to the meetings. Heaven came down and hundreds were truly born again. We counted 1,000 cards for healing, but hundreds were prayed for in the press of the crowd without a card. More importantly, 2,000 decision cards were given out.

God took control; it was out of our hands. I stood in the name of the Most High God, and he then took over. It was truly a revival. Jesus became the victor. The liberating gospel set the masses free. A great light began to dawn on the huge crowds. The gospel, once neglected, or hidden beneath 1,000 years of religious tradition, became of interest to the people. Many lives hanging by a thread were marvellously healed. We scattered the fragments of the bread of life to the town, and thousands of starving souls grasped it. This Republican stronghold was wonderfully stirred by the gospel. A cyclone of power from heaven hit the district. The people could hardly sit still, as they were moved by the glorious presence of God. Thousands were seeing, feeling and hearing of great demonstrations of the power of God.

There were packed gospel meetings in Republican areas near Crossmaglen. In the Donegal Road in Belfast, on the edge of the notorious Nationalist Falls Road, the mission hall had to remove a wall to get the crowds in. The side hall was packed with weeping sinners. Many miracles happened. In Lisburn, a predominantly Loyalist town, the crowds stood outside the gospel hall. It was the largest gathering ever seen in the church building. A woman who had been in a wheelchair for seven years walked down the street pushing her wheelchair home, a blind man could see, and a deaf and dumb girl could shout and speak normally again. Dozens were converted to Christ.

Soon news of this remarkable move of God went around the world. I did not encourage publicity, but the news got out. It was carried not only all over the UK but was even reported in Sweden and Germany. Also in Australia, New Zealand, the South Seas, the USA and South Africa magazines told the same remarkable stories.

AN IRA LEADER

At the end of one precious service, where our lovely Jesus had saved and healed so many, a smart, well-dressed gentleman with a soft Irish voice stood at the door talking with me. He thanked me for coming, even though the English were never welcomed there. I later discovered that he was believed to be among the IRA's top brass. He told me he had no time anymore for the church. When I pointed out that Christ loved us all, he replied in a near-whisper, 'I am beyond redemption. The things I have done cannot be forgiven.' I then told him that Jesus said, 'I will in no wise cast any out who come unto me.' He seemed to think deeply for a moment, then went out into the darkness of the night alone. Even terrorists are being challenged by this revival.

The interest and power increased nightly. A wave of spiritual joy swept over the people in many meetings, as the gospel freed them, sealed them and healed them! The new-born souls in their hundreds went everywhere telling others, 'Look what good things he has done for me – he will do the same for you!'

Love never fails. The great lesson God has taught me in this new staggering revival is that his love is unfailing – he just wants us to spread it. Obedience is also at the heart of the revival: we must be willing to stick our necks out, to dare, to risk, to go and not question, to work with singleness of purpose.

The Master is calling us to greater victories. Who will enlist? Who will obey? Who will beat back the powers of darkness? He has promised, 'I will rebuke the devourer for your sakes.' Our power in Ireland was the atoning blood, the merits of Jesus Christ alone. This is why miracles happened night after night.

As we left one area after a great revival like this, which shook the whole town and the district for miles around, newspaper boys on their deliveries shouted 'Hallelujah!' in the streets at us. People waved to us from the footpaths. At the petrol station the manageress told us that her relatives had been miraculously healed. People called out to us, 'Come back again soon!'

As I was about to return to England at the end of the Irish crusade, I was questioned by the police. They asked me, 'Which areas have you been to? What were you doing with crowds of people in Republican ghettoes? What was the purpose of your visit? Why were you mixing with terrorist sympathizers?' My answers are probably in a police computer somewhere, and I expect it blows a fuse every time they call up my file! I said I went to convert the people to Christ, to deliver them from demons, to heal their sicknesses by the power of Christ, to reconcile them to God! I went to tell them that nothing is impossible to God. I went to demonstrate the power of the Holy Spirit!

TEMPTING PROVIDENCE?

'Once is enough, Melvin. I mean, you got away with it

21

on one occasion, but it would be tempting Providence to go a second time.' Such was the wisdom offered to me by one Christian. I had just told him of my plan to return to Ireland, and not to the safety of a Protestant or moderate Roman Catholic area, but to a Republican town.

He remonstrated, 'There may be needy people there, but isn't that true of every town and city in Europe?' He sighed deeply. 'But these are highly sensitive areas. They have just burnt down a gospel tent in one of these towns. They are unpredictable, unstable gunmen. It's like sitting on a timebomb!'

I quietly replied, 'I've made up my mind. The plans are laid. At this moment, 16,000 gospel invitations are going out personally into every home. We have one of the largest available halls rented ready. We must give these people a chance!'

Exasperated, he told me, 'You're putting a bullet into your own head.'

Such was the kind of discouragement I had to endure in the final two weeks before going back across the water to Ireland.

As I viewed the Irish Sea far below as I flew to Belfast, I was reminded of Holman Hunt's famous painting of Christ in the orchard knocking gently on the door of man's heart. Weeds had grown around the door-frame, symbolizing the neglected heart and lost soul of man. These Irish people were neglected, and centuries of fear, prejudice, tradition and misunderstanding had sealed their fate. It was time that God knocked on the door of their hearts clearly. He had told me to take the living gospel message, with miraculous demonstration and power, to the devil's territory. God was saying, 'The devil has no right to their lives, families, homes or futures.' In

Hunt's painting Christ's feet were pointing down the road in the other direction. He would not always wait, knocking at that door. He would soon move on to other men, other nations, other peoples, other fields. Now was the time to reach the Republican Irish people with a new, powerful revelation of the love of Christ.

As the plane began to descend over Ulster's green fields and white farmhouses, I wondered why I had received so much discouragement about this second crusade from my fellow Christian leaders. Where were those who were willing to enter the demon-infested valleys of this world? Where were those who would follow daringly in Jesus' footsteps, break new ground, take a risk, stick out their necks, have a go, even go 'where angels fear to tread'?

There I was, once more on the edge of this virgin, unreached territory, these 'out of bounds' villages, communities and towns dominated by the Sinn Fein philosophy.

God spoke clearly to me: 'Tell them about My death, burial and resurrection. You are My messenger. Let them know that I care, that I love them. You have this ministry invested in you. The same power that was in Me 2,000 years ago in Galilee is in you. You cannot fail. Dry the tears of the sorrowing. Tell them I am the Bread of Life. Tell them to repent. You must do all you can, and I will do all I can.'

I was so attentive to what God was saying to me that I became oblivious to my surroundings. The stewardess was saying, 'It's time to get off the aircraft, sir.' I hadn't even noticed that we had landed. The bemused stewardess said, 'It's Belfast, sir. We have arrived.' Thanking her, I donned my hat and went down the exit steps from the plane, muttering the words from John's Gospel which God had burned into my brain: 'I must work the works of Christ, while it is day: for the night cometh, when no man can work.'

Soon a friend was driving me from Belfast International Airport towards the border with the Republic. Close to the customs posts a Southern Irish pastor bundled me into his van, and I then discovered the difference between Ulster roads and the Republic's highways. There were potholes and bumps everywhere! Eventually we arrived at the small border town, 40 miles from the worst trouble spots in the north.

The pastor told me that a well-known youth of the town, only 19 years of age, had gone up to help the IRA only a few weeks ago, and had been shot by the British soldiers. Half the town had turned out for his funeral. Before coming to Ireland I had asked that the publicity for the crusade should not contain any references to Britain or to the fact that I am English, since anti-British feelings were very strong here. However, the printer had made a mistake and had left in a mention of my nationality! So everyone knew an Englishman was coming to some high-profile public meetings!

I arrived at the large public hall in this small town on the west coast of Ireland. By 7.45 p.m. the service had not even started. People were coming in late and slowly, often asking many questions outside before venturing into the meeting. It was like trying to get the people inside a spaceship going to Mars! We finally started 30 minutes late, with about 90 people present. I was being supported in this crusade by a tiny fellowship of twelve folk. They were excited that as many as 90 had turned up. I was used to seeing far larger gatherings of people, but in recent months God had been saying to me, 'Don't get used to dynamic results. Don't think that it is yourself from whom this gift comes. Don't seek for just more of My power – seek *My presence*. All else will follow from My being with you!'

A PIONEER SITUATION

As I stood before this small crowd of folk, I realized that they had all struggled with their inherited traditions and inhibitions just to be there. I realized what a special gift God had put in my hands. Here was a pioneer situation. The resources of heaven were behind me, God's covenant blessings were mine. Jesus stood with me as I stood in his presence and anointing. God never sponsors flops. I could not fail in him.

Soon that little audience was to see the incredible power of intercessory prayer. The singing was lacklustre, except for the few young believers from the tiny supporting fellowship – no one else knew the new hymns of Graham Kendrick and Chris Bowater. I realized that they could not truly worship and enjoy God until they had been delivered by the all-powerful gospel of Christ.

As I stood to introduce the crusade, I told them about the Sunday School children who were told by their teacher that they must write to and pray for missionaries in far-off countries – but they should not expect an answer from the missionaries, as they were very, very busy people. Then little Sammy wrote:

Dear Rev. Smith, Missionary,
I am praying for you, but I don't expect an answer . . .

Your friend Sammy.

Southern Irish folk love a joke, and they were in fits of laughter. The ice was broken.

Then I launched into my gospel message, pointing out, as Luther had said, that there are only two sets of people in the world – sinners, who think they are righteous, and the righteous, who think they are sinners. What side of the fence were they on? People could not be saved by man-made religion, but only by God's great mercy. People had to believe in the sufficiency of Christ's atoning blood; they had to believe on the Word of his promise. I explained that sin was essentially pride, ingratitude to our Maker, and the self-gratification of our own minds and bodies. It was rebellion against our rightful owner, God. It was missing the mark of his standards, breaking his law, defiling and polluting ourselves in his sight, shutting our ears to his wisdom, and being guilty at his judgement seat. I urged them finally to heed the words of Mother Teresa of Calcutta to Malcolm Muggeridge, then a hardened atheist: 'You must repent to come into God's joy and Kingdom.'

CONVICTION AND POWER

Soon 50 or more people were kneeling and weeping – some quietly, others audibly. They had been overcome by a sweep of conviction and power from heaven. Within 30 minutes, half the congregation was yearning to be in the Kingdom, and many were already feeling the Kingdom in their souls.

People began to cry out. This was quite unplanned. These were not an excited charismatic crowd, but simply sinners reaching out to God. This went on for some time. Finally we counselled and spoke personally to people as much as we could, but there were so few mature Christians present and so many people needing counselling that we were overwhelmed. But God was falling on these people, and many of them for the first time made a personal friendship with our Lord Jesus Christ. Our Almighty God was answering by fire.

I began to pray for people. The parents of a tiny boy named Sean told me that the finest Dublin doctors had said he would never be able to sit up, let alone stand or walk. I prayed for him – my heart was melted by his sweet, Irish green eyes. I moved on. God was healing many people. A deaf lady could hear my voice. The omnipotent, omnipresent God was with us. People who had run away from God were now running back to him: the rebels were coming home.

But why was this happening among these people, at this time, when they had never been open to God before? That is a question I have often asked myself since, and I still don't know the answer. But there was no doubt that it was God's hour. We were borne along by the Holy Ghost and felt the Divine voice amongst us. We were bathed in a flood of God's glory.

One lady who had been prayed for threw away her two sticks and danced in the street outside the public hall. Men came from the local bars when they heard about the healings. People were soon clapping and cheering God's signs and acts, in a Republican town! Amazing!

Then someone touched my shoulder, and I turned, and he pointed across to tiny Sean, who was now standing up! It brought the house down!

Hours after the meeting began, we made our weary way back to our digs, in a small guest-house near the sea. What a night! And it was just the beginning!

So it went on. The crowds increased, the miracles proliferated, the news travelled fast. Irish national radio carried the story. People packed the hall.

One night I prayed for a tough-looking, bushy-haired, tall man who was on crutches and in great pain. He didn't say much to me; he looked down towards the floor most of the time. He was truly suffering. His lined, swollen face and slightly unkempt appearance spoke of someone who had been through the mill.

Suddenly, like a flash, God visited him. We stepped back. Sweat appeared on his brow. He began to smile and dropped his crutches. 'The pain's gone!' he cried. 'It's gone – I can't feel a thing!' He began to flex his muscles and bend his body, very slowly and cautiously, as if he could hardly believe it. Soon he was walking up and down the aisles. The people were delighted by this man's healing. I asked the local pastor who was helping me in this mission who this man was.

As if to tell me some closely guarded secret, he whispered in my ear, 'He's a big Sinn Fein man – a local hero. He was beaten up and nearly kicked to death 18 months ago on the border by British troops, when discovered scouting for the IRA. He came back broken up and has been in that awful condition ever since.' He went out healthy and painless, his bones knitting together like a little two-year-old's. He was now a committed follower of our Lord Jesus, a new-born baby, just starting out, a new creature in Christ.

This is the work of the Divine Communicator. By miracles Jesus reveals the Father's love: 'What he sees the Father do, he does.' At the end of the crusade, before I headed home, we held a supper for all the people who had been converted and healed. I told the 250 people who turned up how they could grow in God's grace and in faith. What stories they had to tell! They could fill a book alone, from that one revival.

A BREAKTHROUGH

This remarkable breakthrough in a Republican area proves that God wants his people to take his power on to the streets, into hostile territory. There is no such thing as a 'no go area' for the gospel. It is the key to open the hardest of hearts. People everywhere long for the Living God. They don't need dry, irrelevant theology, but a gospel of truth, reality, joy, power and deliverance. One mighty miracle is worth more than any amount of powerless theology. It is Bible truth that sets people free.

No terrorist, no cultural barrier, no gun or bomb, no powers of this world, no evil can prevent the supernatural power of the cross, of the bleeding Lamb of God, Jesus Christ, from conquering hearts and minds with his love. The media ask, 'What is this message that won in Ireland?' It is this: 'By the sacrifice of himself, Christ put away sin.' I was merely his mouthpiece. It was the wounds, bruises and suffering of Christ that won men and women to the glorious Kingdom of God.

We saw hundreds of Irish people abandon their old lifestyle – they gave up gambling, superstition, drunkenness, smoking, occult practices and pornographic literature. Many people gave up adulterous relationships, squared their debts and paid their bills. This was all the result of the old but ever-new message of the cross. The genuine gospel of Jesus swept through their towns, cleansing, washing, humbling, changing, transforming, re-creating, rehabilitating, remaking and revitalizing!

3

UNLIKELY PEOPLE AND PLACES

The present revival is reaching some unlikely places and transforming the lives of many individuals. When God works in power, there are always surprises.

GIPSIES AND BIKERS

The Gipsies have for a long time been unreached by the gospel, but now thousands of them are finding Christ. I was recently in three new Gipsy churches in Cambridgeshire. At one service 100 people were baptized.

The revival has also had an amazing effect on the wild Biker gangs. A number of Biker churches have started up. These wild people, who had been tied up with violence, the occult, and New Age movement, drink and drugs are being set free by Jesus. A new moral revival has begun amongst the Biker gangs.

I was preaching one night in a posh Assemblies of God church. Suddenly I heard the sound of motorbikes outside. It sounded like a hundred machines! A few minutes later the church doors banged open, and in came line upon line of these tough, rough Bikers. There were about 50 of them in all, including a couple of girls. All were dressed in black, with leathers, chains, swastikas and high, heavy boots on.

The worried pastor jumped up and asked me, 'What are we going to do?'

'Well, let's try and get them converted!' I replied.

Through my 20-minute gospel sermon they were very quiet and listened intently. Then when I made the appeal, before anyone else could respond, suddenly all the Bikers raised a hand in the air. This was to signify that they wanted to know Christ as the Lord of their lives. The church was crammed with these big fellows – they were weeping, sighing deeply and crying out. The church members gave them scriptures, counselled them, advised them and hugged them.

Since then nearly 1,000 Bikers have been converted. Biker gospel rallies have been held. On their bikes they now have Bible texts instead of swastikas. I once rode with a Biker at 70 m.p.h. down the M4. 'Prepare to meet thy God' was the motto on his bike – I nearly did that day!

RAIN FROM HEAVEN

I was once invited to hold a mission in a certain town at a time when there was much greater potential for missions elsewhere. It seemed unlikely that revival could come to this particular town, but God impressed me more and more to go there. We used a tent for the campaign, and night after night it rained. Outside, the ground became a quagmire; people trying to get to the tent slipped and skidded in the mud. The local newspapers were antagonistic and fault-finding, and money was short for publicity. The situation seemed very unpromising.

But suddenly, just as I was about to give up, the breakthrough happened: heaven came down and the whole community was shaken by miracles! The papers changed their minds and crowds packed the tent. The rain still came down, but the rain from heaven came down heavier. Miracle after miracle flowed, and hundreds were converted. By the end of the month over 2,000 had been saved. We extended the crusade twice. Wheelchairs were piled up after being emptied.

In the town there was a club for agoraphobia sufferers. Many housewives had this terrible fear and could never leave the house by themselves. Through the mission so many of these people were healed of this sickness that the agoraphobic club was closed down! The Lord delivered them from all their fear! 'The perfect love of God casts out fear.'

GREAT TRAIN ROBBER FINDS CHRIST

We have an amazing God, an amazing Jesus, an amazing Saviour and Healer! I can bring to mind so many examples of his miraculous power. I was recently touring the West Country, visiting new churches which I had seen planted during my ministry there over the past few years. One wet and blustery Sunday afternoon, between large morning and evening meetings, I squeezed in a visit to a small church in a village near the coast. There were about 50 people in the congregation, and during the service ten people gave their hearts to the Lord, which was most encouraging for this small fellowship.

At the end of the service I prayed for the sick. Then, after shaking hands with people and drinking a quick cup of tea, I was heading for the door. One of the church leaders stopped me. 'Do you know who was converted today?' he asked me.

'What do you mean?' I asked, not knowing what to expect.

'Today,' he told me, 'one of the Great Train Robbers came to Christ!'

I caught my breath as I remembered the notorious robbery of the Royal Mail in Buckinghamshire in 1963. This man, it appeared, had been one of the ringleaders. He had been in prison for many years, and had become asthmatic. He had come along to the church 'to give it a try', and had found Christ. He also had a wonderful release from his asthma. That was a miracle!

HEAVY DRINKER CONVERTED

Then there is my friend Bert in Portsmouth: a living testimony to the miraculous power of Christ today. Bert was a heavy drinker. He spent his days in the pub and believed in nothing – not even in himself. One evening his wife announced that she was going out. Bert was puzzled, as she tended to be a homebird who rarely went out by herself, but his wife explained about the leaflet which had come through the door, and that she wanted to see the evangelist and be prayed for. Bert laughed and went off to the pub, but when he arrived home that night he found his wife joyful and singing hymns.

The same thing happened every night that week. Bert was mystified by the change in his wife, yet he resisted all her attempts to persuade him to come to a meeting. At last the crusade ended and I moved on to another town. But Bert's wife had bought one of the tapes that were on sale at the crusade – a tape of Alan Pimlott, the renowned soloist from Norwich. She played this wonderful tape almost non-stop. Bert heard it when he got up in the morning; he heard it when he came home from the pub each night. Finally he was touched by it. Two elders from the local Christian Fellowship prayed for Bert, and he was converted. A lifetime's habit of heavy drinking stopped immediately; he was set free!

I often see Bert when I preach in Portsmouth: a short, well-built man singing lustily with the Langstone Fellowship singers – a witness of the change wrought by the risen Christ, a modern miracle of Christ Jesus our Lord!

A DOCTOR'S REPORT

I have this confirmation of the miraculous from a respected medical practitioner, Dr Q. M. Adams, MRCS, LRCP, FRSM:

> I have attended Rev Melvin Banks' missions on several occasions, indeed some of my own patients, including a young farmer's wife, have been amazingly cured. This particular person, whose condition I knew well, was suffering greatly from a spinal condition which was deteriorating despite all my efforts. After Rev Banks' laying on of hands and prayers she was astonishingly and instantaneously healed, and has never suffered since. She can now run, jump, and lie down painlessly. There are others I know of who were also cured completely. I have personally checked many cases and am aware of the genuine illnesses of many of the people who have visited Mr Banks. There are, without doubt, many miracles in his services.
>
> I sat in a crowded chapel in Cornwall not long ago, and saw a blind man led in. On investigating the case I discovered that the man had been blind for at least eight years, and had travelled 80 miles, over remote country roads, to get to the service.

Later in the meeting, as crippled people were seen joyfully and painlessly walking, and deaf people regained their hearing, this man started to describe the cross on the far end of the wall of the chapel, the height of the windows, the colours of the flowers decorating the church. It was without doubt all real and genuine.

POLICE CALLED OUT

I was holding a mission a few years ago in a town in the North of England. Five newspapers reported the sensational scenes that took place. The local bingo hall manageress was quoted as saying, 'I may as well close up; I have done virtually no business this last two weeks.' The police had to be called out to control the traffic, for crowds of people were travelling to the services as news of the miracles spread. This was a mining community hard hit by the recession and with a very low rate of churchgoing; these were tough, sceptical, unemotional people. That was a miracle for today!

In another town people pulled off the church gates to get in, and climbed the scaffolding around the church to look through the windows. In Gloucester, people stood in pouring rain for three hours, sat in the windows, stood outside and crammed the doorways in their eagerness to hear the message we were bringing.

REVIVAL CLOSES A CINEMA

The Oxford Dictionary defines a miracle as 'anything beyond human power and deviating from the common action of the laws of nature'.

35

C. S. Lewis defined a miracle as 'an interference with nature by supernatural power'. It is the supernatural activity of God. I have seen miracle after miracle – incredible miracles, extraordinary miracles, stunning miracles! I have seen the conquest of debilitating diseases; I have seen the beds of the sick and the paralysing emptied; I have seen a dead person raised back to life!

I sometimes pass through a little town in Lincolnshire where I held one of my first crusades. God had swept in with revival power, and a church was established. I pass what was once a cinema, but is now a supermarket, and every time I pass I say to myself, 'There is a testimony to the miracles of God today.' During my ministry there, the cinema owner was saved and became a strong disciple of Christ. This was 28 years ago, when the cinema was much more popular than it is now. But that woman decided to close her cinema down so that films of questionable morality would no longer be shown in the area. The town became a healthier and happier place, bearing witness to God's good work today. That was a miracle of God! His supernatural power moving in revival closed that cinema down!

Augustine said, 'I should not be a Christian but for the miracles.' Miracles evoke wonder, awe and even the fear of the Almighty God. Miracles demonstrate the explosive power of the Almighty!

LIKE A MIGHTY WIND

One man was among the many who were unable to get in to the revival meeting in Sprotborough, near Doncaster, since the hall was packed out. He was on crutches, but they could not find one more inch to accommodate anyone else. As the people worshipped God, the Spirit came in like a mighty wind, flooding the whole audience. Not only did 100 people get converted, but sticks, wheelchairs and other equipment were left behind in the hall, and many on the streets outside were healed. The man on crutches was unable to see the meeting inside, but he felt the power and joy of God; his pain was eased and divine heat went through his body. He was soon dancing along the pavement, his wife holding his crutches. The passers by were utterly amazed!

DEAF GIRL HEALED

One lady in a Northampton town could not get in to the meetings, as the crowd was so densely packed. Not one more person could gain admittance. It was so hot that some were almost fainting. Many were sitting on each other's knees! The lady had a little deaf girl who had never heard any sounds before. She stayed outside on the pathway to the hall, listening to the wonderful worship, through the open doors. Then as the gospel was proclaimed, the Holy Spirit fell upon the whole crowd. Inside the hall a woman's goitre vanished. The church worker who was beside her saw it disappear into thin air and fainted at the sight!

People were converted and healed all over the building. The lady with the deaf girl could feel the power of the Spirit even outside! Suddenly the child turned her head back and forth, tossing and turning, looking up, trying to talk, pointing at the lorries passing by. She put her hands over her ears – the noise of the passing traffic was too much for her!

A few weeks later it was confirmed by an ear and throat specialist that she could hear perfectly!

SHETLAND REVIVAL

When I led a crusade in the Shetlands, huge crowds came to the big theatre in Lerwick. After this we went out to Mossbank, a tiny community of crofters, hill people, fishermen and oilmen. When I drove down the dimly lit main street, I wondered how many people would come from such a small but affluent community.

In the dark we got out of the car in the small car park. Ours was the only car there! The car park remained empty till five minutes before the service. But soon crowds flocked through the door of the hall, filling up the seats and soon demanding extra seating. Many were non-church folk; in fact there was no church in that whole community. We had come into the desert, and it was beginning to blossom like the rose.

The people had difficulty picking up the hymns and new choruses of the revival, since they weren't used to singing in religious meetings. But then I preached the Word of God, and remarkably, the people wept and came through to Christ all over the place.

There was a man with Parkinson's disease, badly paralysed and uncoordinated in his walk. He was known throughout the south Shetlands and was considered an incurable case. Suddenly his body was straightened and he was able to walk without shaking and with proper coordination. A wonderful miracle began for him. The hall was in uproar! These reserved, cautious, unemotional, shy islanders were clapping and gasping with amazement as God worked amongst them in supernatural power.

The revival grew, and soon the whole of the Shetland Isles knew about the gospel and miracles of Christ. A large portion of the population flocked to the meetings.

THE REVIVAL REACHES MUSLIMS

A Baptist church in central Nottingham invited me to lead a mission. There were many large, prosperous churches in that city area, and so competition was strong for this little church. Few people were being saved through its work. Its newish building was huge but almost empty, since the congregation was small. They were faithful people, but they had almost given up on the vast unsaved community around them, which included large numbers of Muslims and Rastafarians. In the wisdom of man I would have chosen to work with a large, thriving Pentecostal congregation. But God's wisdom said, 'No, go to that tiny Baptist church, and I will send you a visitation of the Holy Spirit.'

Up to 100 people came forward nightly in the great crusade. People flocked to the meetings – not from the wealthy suburbs, but from the immediate locality. They were mostly working-class folk, many of them from the ethnic minorities. It was a local move of God.

One night a tall, well-dressed Muslim gentleman came in. He was a big printer in the city who was respected in his local mosque. He had never been in a Christian church. Drawn by the sounds and sights of miracles, he wept at the front, seeking God for his salvation. Then at the close of the service, there I was – an old Pentecostal preacher – dancing around in the aisle, hugging a Muslim, shouting, 'Your sins are forgiven!' And he was shouting, 'I'm forgiven! The Lord has saved me!' All this in a respectable Baptist church!

During the amazing revival meetings in a church in Balsall Heath recently, so many Muslims were crowding into the church that the whole district was amazed by the scenes. Prior to the mission almost no one from the huge local Muslim community ever came to the church. The members of the well-attended chapel were mainly black and white Christians who came from outside the area, some travelling several miles to the meetings. But they knew that evangelism is not real unless it's local, so they really wanted to reach the vast local Muslim populace.

If Christians are serious about evangelizing this society, we must try to reach the 2 million non-white neighbours on our doorstep. Most British churches have completely given up on them. But they are real people. They have hearts and feelings just like anyone else. They are not all bigoted and unreachable. They will respond to the love of God, and especially to signs and wonders. If we do nothing for these folk, our denominational churches will come under God's judgement. We must put our house in order, and reach out with passion and love to these desperate people.

In Balsall Heath the Muslims were building a mosque to seat an estimated 5,000 people just opposite the Gospel Chapel. What a challenge!

On the first night of the mission only a row or two of Muslims turned up. The chapel was full of Christians and unsaved white folk. But the Muslim people were amongst the first to ask for salvation and the gospel at the end of the service. One big fellow, wearing the traditional oblong-shaped hat, came off his crutches within seconds of being prayed for! God was revealing himself to them by signs and wonders, and the fear of God came on them all. The next night half the church was filled with Muslims. They started to put our posters, with the name of Jesus in large print at the top, up in their shop windows throughout the district. By the end of the crusade the Christians could hardly get into their own church, so many Muslims packed the place out.

Then came an unusual invitation. I was asked to come to the mosque to talk with the leaders. I discussed this with one of the pastors, who was reluctant to let me go. However, I went, and was given the 'red carpet' treatment. I was sure God was guiding me to go right into the 'lions' den' to preach the all-powerful gospel of Christ. I was more warmly received there than in some Christian churches, which want nothing to do with the miraculous, supernatural power of the Lord. But these people were so open.

On the walls of the mosque were pictures of the Ayatollah Khomeini. 'What have I got myself into?' I thought. 'Will they get the knives out in a minute?' But hot tea, Bangladeshi cakes, sweets and other Asian delights filled the table. I was shown to a comfortable seat. There was bowing, hand-shaking and hearty smiles. They appreciated my willingness to come.

We ate and chatted about our beliefs. We started at the creation and moved on to Moses and the Ten Commandments, the sovereignty of God, the Old Testament law, the Psalms and Isaiah.

'God is all-powerful,' the mullah declared.

'Jesus is alive, and he is coming again,' I replied. They all excitedly agreed.

So the two-hour conversation went on. It was all very civilized, and we talked about Jesus a great deal. I prayed for them in his name, and some of them were freed from physical pains. God revealed himself to them. It was a remarkable afternoon: I had spoken to them about the love of Christ and I had seen his power manifested mightily among them.

In revival surprising doors open, and converts are made in the most unusual of places!

A CHURCH IS REBORN

Following a successful crusade in Blackpool in 1986, I noticed that something needed to be done in South Blackpool, which was almost untouched by Spirit-filled evangelism. I was pleased when I was invited to work in a tiny church there.

A short while before this, two elderly Christian ladies had moved into the area. One day they went to a local mission hall, built of fine Lancashire stone in the 1930s. Now it was dilapidated and empty and was having its closing service! A Muslim had offered a huge sum for this building near the seafront, where property prices were sky high. He wanted to turn it into a mosque.

The two ladies nearly fainted when they heard the church leader (an old man who had now given up) announce to the tiny congregation that this was to be the last service to be held there. When he told them at the door that the building was to be sold to the Muslims, they argued fiercely that this was 'madness'!

He was taken aback by their courage and audacity. They told him bluntly that they would not let the church close. They stood against his utter negativeness and his complete surrender to years of decline, prayer-lessness and defeatism. The little old ladies argued away, even threatening to sit on the premises rather than let him sell it to the Muslims. He reluctantly agreed that if they would support the church, he would try again.

The story is a long one, but eventually the old fellow handed the church over to a young man full of the Holy Ghost. He invited me along to help his little struggling band. Miracles happened, revival broke out, the church was relaunched and God gave it a fresh foundation. Today it has so many members that it needs a larger building. The minister now works full time. This church has touched hundreds of lives in the local area.

EVEN THE DEAD ARE RAISED!

With an anxious face, the steward waved his hand to attract my attention in the middle of the meeting.

The local hall of this small West Country town was packed with 250 people; they had come to the meeting after hearing about signs, wonders and miracles in other nearby communities. The meeting was going well, and the people were singing with real gusto. The abundant prayer which had preceded the mission was bringing the blessing down. Many sick people were waiting to hear the Word of God and to receive healing.

Then there was this disturbance at the back. I could spy a man right at the top of the aisle lying on the floor. A lady was kneeling over him, trying to pump air into his lungs. It looked serious to me. But, of course, I deal with tens of thousands of sick folk in meetings. Many are brought in on respirators; many come from the emergency wards of hospitals, often with nurses. I am used to seeing seriously ill people, so I was not too worried, and left the matter to my excellent staff.

After ten minutes, there were four people around the motionless man, who was still lying on his side. A note from the worried steward told me things were not good. The man had died! The lady who had worked on him for so long was a registered nurse, and she advised calling an ambulance urgently. He had no heart-beat, no breathing, no pulse!

I ordered no ambulance. The vision of laughing medics carrying away a corpse hit me square between the eyes. I could imagine the newspaper headlines: 'Man carried dead from divine healing meeting!'

But more than this, I felt Jesus' compassion for the man, who had come to the meeting in such a state and yet had died before being ministered to. I could see that the devil was trying to cause havoc through this, to discredit Almighty God in the eyes of the world. The honour of God was at stake!

I did not want the hundreds of lost sinners to get worried; I didn't want them to become preoccupied with the thought of the dead man at the back of the hall, and so to forget the gospel message and Christ's challenge. So, staying at the front, I prayed a prayer of deliverance and resurrection, pointing to the back, and I added an earnest second prayer silently.

I went on with the meeting telling the people how they could be saved through Jesus Christ. What an atmosphere! It seemed as if the whole congregation wanted to get saved!

After I had prayed, I saw that the man had revived! He stood up and walked about slowly. I couldn't get the stewards back to the front; they seemed to be lost in this miracle at the back. The nurse told me later, 'I tried to pump him, to get air into him. But he was gone! He was cold, he was dead. The morgue seemed the only place for him. I can't believe it!'

Glory came down on the healing line. Everyone seemed to be cured that night. Christ was exalted above all, and scores were converted. It was a night of Bible miracles and supernatural Christianity.

CLOWN FINDS A NEW JOY

In physical stature I am a small man, but the former clown Jimmy Scott was tiny compared even to me. Now ageing, he had many marvellous stories to tell of a glamorous life on the sawdust ring of the circus. In his time he had worked for Bertram Mills, Chipperfield's and Billy Smart's. He had been on TV many times.

With his wide travels, Jimmy had never been a great churchgoer. However, like most travelling people, there was a 'quiet fear of God' in him. Then came my crusade that packed the Music Hall in the rural town of Boston. Hundreds of sick folk came. Jimmy, now crippled with arthritis, came along for healing. But he also came to understand that he needed to become one of God's children. Soon he became wonderfully converted. He joined a local Christian fellowship and never missed a meeting amongst God's people. As a clown it had been his job to make people laugh, but now he found a deep inner joy he had never had before. He had appeared four times before royalty, but now he had met our Lord Jesus Christ, the King of the universe, who changed his life completely.

When he got healed he did a few acts for us, including some gymnastics on the platform, to the joy and laughter of the audience.

The clown had found a new life. God is always at work and surprises are his trademark.

RELEASED FROM PARALYSIS

The local papers carried the story of the young woman in her thirties who had been partially paralysed from birth. She was a familiar figure in Tiverton in Devon, her body bent over as she struggled to walk. She was one of the thousands who came to the ten-day-long mission in the town. The whole district for miles around talked of the 'strange' happenings and the miracles.

The young woman had a miraculous cure by the Holy Spirit's power. She could soon walk properly, and before long she learned to ride a bicycle!

HEALED FROM MENTAL ILLNESS

One day recently, during a revival in an East Coast town, there was a knock at the door of the house I was staying in. A young man stood before me. I asked him in and we got talking. Although he was so young, he had had several nervous breakdowns. He had been everywhere for help: doctors, psychologists and every passing ministry. But after 15 minutes of earnest prayer he received joy, release and peace from God. The guilt and fear of years vanished. My heart went out to that frightened, brave young man. Gently I led him to Christ. It was, after all, the Lord Jesus who said: 'Come to me, all of you who are weary and burdened, and I will give you rest. Take my yoke upon you and learn from me, for I am gentle and humble in heart, and you will find rest for your souls. For my yoke is easy and my burden is light' (Matthew 11:28-29). The young man has remained well and committed to Christ.

4

RURAL REVIVAL

Recently I led a mission at Hittisleigh Chapel, between Tiverton and Oakhampton in Devonshire. The local people are normally reserved, but their response to the mission was astonishing. The meetings were packed out, nearly 100 people were converted and many people were healed of sicknesses.

People wept. Big farmers broke down. Young people called upon God. A few walked out of the meetings when they found it was too much.

People who hadn't been to church for decades queued up to get a seat. I called upon the thronged congregations in words of Colossians 3:5-7: 'Renounce impurity, evil desires, lust, sexual immorality, greed and idolatry. Yearn to be in the body of Christ. Weep rivers of tears till you have found him. Make your dominant ambition God's Kingdom, and his righteousness!' I urged the quiet, attentive crowds to 'Put away rage, malice, slander, filthy language and lying' (Colossians 3:8-9) so that in 'everything he might have supremacy' (Colossians 1:18).

One of the features of the present revival is that it is reaching isolated rural areas, such as parts of Devon, Lincolnshire and Hampshire.

As the media became interested in what was happening, I was interviewed on BBC Radio Devon. Tens of thousands of people heard it. The interviewer, John Reynolds, at first had a sceptical attitude.

John: How long have you been doing this?

Melvin: 30 years ago I filled in for a well-known evangelist. I believed in the miracles of the Bible ...

John: Let me be sceptical it's a load of rubbish, isn't it!

Melvin: It's hard for an unbelieving generation, and a very materialistic, selfish age to believe that anyone can come with a pure motive and do anything for anyone out of a sheer sense of calling and love for people.

I've been here a long time, I've been examined by the media, had a thousand reports ... Even two days ago at the Methodist Chapel, Hittisleigh, a crippled woman was one of many who were remarkably healed by our Lord. Yesterday she waltzed into the service, no pain, no stick, no crippled condition, absolutely thrilled ... These things happen today. It is Jesus Christ who heals. It is the Bible coming alive today.

John: So you say it is God ...?

Melvin: I am a poor channel – I'm not a very good preacher. But I do have God's authority. God has to use people, and I've put myself at God's disposal. He must use someone. He wants to bring his comfort, healing and life. The gift of healing is for the church. The Bible is full of healing, and these gifts are given by God for all time, yesterday, today and forever. He uses ordinary people – fishermen, tax-gatherers, labourers, dyers and tent-makers – to convert, to heal, to deliver, to bring the life-transforming gospel to multitudes. He is still using ordinary folk. I was a bricklayer, Smith-

48

Wigglesworth was a plumber, Stephen Jefferies was a coal-miner, Reinhardt Bonnke was an office worker, Dr Cho was a soldier. And such men God is using to shake the earth! God called me, gifted me, anointed me, gave me power from on high and used me to set multitudes of the captives and sick free!

John: Why has he not gifted the church? They could really do with this sort of PR at the moment!

Melvin: Well, I am part of the church. I'm serving with the church. Being saved, I belong to the church, for it is not, of course, a property but a people, not a building or system but a blood-washed people. It is not materialistic but spiritual, not political but mystical. I am a part of this glorious body.

John: Why aren't these gifts in plenty in British churches?

Melvin: There are many more gifts in the young churches of Malaysia, Africa, the South Sea Islands, than in Europe. Maybe this is because we are too professional, too liberal, and too many ministers have sold out the anointing of God, sold out to earthly things. We must be more spiritual, more prayerful and more obedient to God.

John: How much does it cost?

Melvin: There is no payment for healing – everything is free. We sometimes take an offering (often we don't even do that). We don't solicit for funds. The offering is of free will. As I often say, the churches that never see any miracles take an offering, so we have every right to, seeing we are delivering all the biblical gifts and benefits of the scripture and not selling the people short!

John: How important is belief in this matter?

Melvin: I ask people to believe in the Bible and to believe in God. People tend to paint a picture of England as being full of rampant unbelief, but there is a lot of latent faith, far more goodwill and faith around than we imagine. There are a lot of people out there who may have fallen away from the church, but they are only a step away. Many sceptics come to my meetings, and soon come to faith. They hear the Word of God, and faith forms and grows, and they lose their doubts. Faith is not a difficult thing. Faith can come into being or be revived. Romans 12:3 says, 'we all have a measure of faith', and all our lives can be changed by faith.

John: Isn't 'miracles' a strong word in your publicity?

Melvin: The Bible is a miracle book. Without the supernatural, Christianity is just like any other religion. The divinity of Christ, the mystical, all-powerful work of the Holy Spirit makes it different from any other faith or teaching.

John: What happens in a miracle service? What sort of pressures are on people?

Melvin: There is a beautiful worship service, a reading from the Bible, a short sermon on the cross and the blood of Christ. Then we make a challenge for people to trust Christ. There is no undue pressure to be converted, but it is the greatest of all decisions. Then people fill a little card in, so we know what is wrong with them. Nothing is done in the corner. We don't look for the media or mass publicity, but neither do we shun it. We are not ashamed of the gospel of Christ, and we boldly declare his power, promises and miracles before the world. Everyone has hands laid on them prayerfully and personally, and God's power is so often released. Mighty miracles often happen.

John: Now you have come in here today, you are going to talk about your successes, but what about the failures?

Melvin: I never claim, of course, that everyone is healed. That would be ridiculous. God can heal everyone – there are nights when it seems everyone gets healed. Other times only 20 per cent seem to respond.

John: Where does belief come in here? Do people have to have strong faith, is it yourself . . .?

Melvin: It's not God's fault if people are not healed, but neither do I ever blame people, or say to people they have not had enough faith. If folk are not apparently healed – and, by the way, I often leave folk with no immediate change, go back a year later and they are healthy and perfect! – but even where people are not cured straight away, I totally blame myself.

John: Is this work exhausting? Do you feel anything when people are healed?

Melvin: Very much. By the end of an evening I am utterly exhausted and drained. The people often feel tremedous power, warmth and spiritual uplift-ment, sometimes almost overwhelming . . .

John: How do you heal ME and other unknown diseases?

Melvin: I pray for a lot of ME in the South Pacific. This disease means people get tired all day, feel very weak and can only work for two hours a day. I first met it in New Zealand, and many folk were healed of it. God can do anything.

John: Why don't you go into hospitals?

Melvin: Well, I do go into hospitals from time to time, if I'm invited, but in meetings you can gather many folk in one place. It could take half a day to travel to one hospital and pray for just one person, when in the same time I could pray for 200 and see most healed, perhaps. You cannot go all over the place praying for individual people. Jesus drew large multitudes and healed them all, the Word of God says. The people also need to hear the Word, which brings faith. So meetings are scriptural, more convenient, helping far more people. And also ambulances actually bring the sick from the hospitals, with nurses with them, to some of my meetings. Faith comes from the Word abiding in you, after hearing it. Faith moves mountains!

John: Can you heal animals? Can I bring Tiddles my cat along?

Melvin: Actually, a gentleman came last night telling me his wife had been wonderfully cured, so could I heal his dog? Animals are the only company which some elderly, lonely people have, so it is serious to them. And God spoke his Word through a donkey in the Bible. And

John Wesley prayed for his horse, and it got healed! God created the animals. He is all-powerful, and he can do these marvellous things even for animals.

John: There are lots of folk, phoning in, Melvin, and one listener has said, 'Healing is from within, and it is little to do with God.'

Melvin: No, it has everything to do with God. Jesus Christ is God; he put on human flesh and came into this world. The Bible tells us he is the great Healer and Saviour. He is the Great Physician who has never lost one case or one patient. We must be careful of certain other types of healing. We must seek Christian biblical healing and be wary of things coming from within or without. Be wary of occult voices and strange phenomena. These things are unsound and unbiblical.

John: Could you be wrong, absolutely 100 per cent wrong?

Melvin: I know for a certain fact that Jesus Christ lives in my heart, that he is my personal Saviour. He is alive. Everyone who repents and believes can have the same certain knowledge and revelation of God. I talk to him each day. We are unworthy and we deserve to die, but he died for us.

John: How do you have a strong belief like that?

Melvin: I have sought him and surrendered to him. 'Seek and you will find,' he promised. I have had a personal experience of God.

John: Ever get depressed?

Melvin: Sometimes I get discouraged with the modern church in Europe and the UK. It's so slow!

Christianity is booming throughout the world, but here the Christians are so often petty, worldly and weak, and don't care about the man in the street. I get frustrated with our churches here. But there are some good ones. Over the years I have worked with some excellent churches. However, most are deadly slow – singing, dancing, celebrating, prophesying, having a good time, but quite removed from the millions of dear, nice unsaved people!

John:　What about the children? How can mentally handicapped people believe?

Melvin:　God loves the children. Jesus said, 'Suffer the little children to come unto me.' They don't need to believe; we can have faith for them. In any case, the simple trust of a child is often far greater than that of most adults. For instance, in Swansea a little boy named Craig was carried into a service. He was unable to move, sit up or communicate. He had no hope, not even a very long expectation of life. Yet, a year later I was in that city again, and there was Craig running about in the aisles. A wonderful change! But even if a child doesn't understand, God loves and knows the child.

John:　So it's one-way traffic.

Melvin:　No, not at all, but sometimes God heals and they believe afterwards. God does not have a regimental attitude to people. Scripture says, 'they believed on him when they saw the miracles that he did.' God reverses his own order because of his nature of supreme love.

John:　Must we always have faith?

Melvin: God doesn't cast us out because we have no faith at the moment. Faith can grow. Faith is not some 'out of the world' experience given to a chosen few. All can believe if we apply ourselves, if we want it. Faith is not a leap into the dark but a leap into the light. Everyone can have faith.

John: How do you fund your tours?

Melvin: There is no payment for healing. All meetings are admission-free. We sometimes take a freewill offering. But the churches who don't believe in miracles take offerings, so why should we not when we are delivering all the biblical goods? However, often there is not an offering taken. The gifts of God are always free!

John: 'How does God select people for healing?' Janet has just rung to ask. Many people are ringing; the lines are getting jammed with questions.

Melvin: I cannot spend ten minutes with each person, but just a touch is enough. Many are healed as they wait. Scripture says, 'Lay hands on the sick and they shall recover.' I believe equally for everyone, whether their healing comes straight away or gradually.

John: What happens when you or your family are sick?

Melvin: My own son had a terrible accident. They said they would have to take his leg off. We prayed, he was healed and needed no amputation. I am not sick, but I often get fatigued and drained. But waiting on God in prayer and soaking myself in God's holy Word refreshes

	me. I rise in the resurrection power of Christ into new energy and the power of the Holy Spirit.
John:	What is going to happen when you die?
Melvin:	I'm going to heaven, John, and you can come with me.
John:	But how do you know?
Melvin:	Because as a sinner I came to Jesus unworthy, unclean, unfit. Yet because Jesus died and rose again, he saved me, and I have the divine certainty that I'm going to meet him one day soon. I'm not going there because of all the wheelchairs I've seen emptied, all the blind seeing, all the deaf hearing, all the crippled walking, all the sick children who've been wonderfully healed, but by grace alone, not by works. It's all the works of the Holy Spirit in any case, the glory belongs to God. He saved us by his blood and Power. He will save the repentant!
John:	What is heaven like?
Melvin:	It's a wonderful place, a huge place. There are trees, walls, flowers, rivers, beautiful things. To me, heaven is the most marvellous city in the universe. It is the best of earth a thousand times magnified.
John:	What is hell like, then?
Melvin:	It's the Nazi camps, the hellish Gulag Sibernian camps, the worst of earth a thousand times magnified.
John:	Why are we here?
Melvin:	We are here to live for the glory of God, to live a life of happiness and fulfilment for others.

John: Why the problems in famine areas? Why are so many dying and starving?

Melvin: There is not a lack of food in our world. Scientists tell us there is enough for everyone in the world to have plenty, but a small corner of the earth selfishly keeps most for itself. This is the politicians' job, not the job of the church. Enoch Powell said, 'The task of the church is not to feed the poor but to teach and preach the gospel.' We must get back to spiritual things, to the power of the gospel. But of course, we should also love and help the poor.

John: Do you believe in reincarnation?

Melvin: No, I don't believe in this. I think it's a ridiculous idea. It's mentioned nowhere in the Bible. It's a type of Hinduism, unfounded and unpractical.

John: Why can't these people have their beliefs too? Why must you be so right all the time?

Melvin: Because the Bible says so, that is our sole authority. No one denies anyone their own belief. I draw more Muslims, Hindus and Sikhs than any other Christian minister in Britain. I love these people, there is no racism in me. I will listen to their story, but I must recommend Jesus Christ as the only way to heaven. He is the answer to man's need. He is our only hope.

John: What a fascinating conversation! What a great morning we have had with Melvin Banks today. I thank all the listeners for ringing in. We have had an overwhelming response. We could go on for hours. We all wish Melvin well on his mission.

John Reynolds was sceptical during the interview, but when the subject of gospel healing was brought up again later, he remarked, 'I believe it now. I am convinced, I'm no longer sceptical towards it.'

This was the BBC broadcast that helped to bring about a revival. As a result of the programme, hundreds poured into the East Devon valleys to get to the meetings. Some people even arrived in the afternoon to get a seat for the evening meeting, which was four to five hours later. It was a remarkable revival!

5

BE A SOUL-WINNER!

Thank God there is beginning to be a slow shift in our nation's values. Perhaps people are tired of seeing so much pain on our television screens and reading about it in our newspapers. Even the unconverted exclaim: 'There must be more to life than this!'

There is! But how will they hear without someone serving the Lord and communicating that message? 'Be bold – be strong – for the Lord your God is with you!'

I am praying for God to give me one million souls in the next few years. Don't forget, the whole gospel for the whole world. Do not add to or subtract from God's Word. The Spirit of God will help and lead you. Open your heart to him! He is seeking you! He is looking for you and he says, 'Go out into the whole world.'

Don't just pray – work, and work hard. There is no time to lose. Be active until Jesus comes. I know that we cannot all be ministers, evangelists, missionaries or teachers. Perhaps you are a mother and housewife; maybe you are a young girl or boy; maybe you are an office or factory worker; a lawyer, doctor, merchant, seaman or farmer. No matter who or what you are, no matter which church you belong to, if you say you believe in God and love God, you'd better be a soul-winner. And if you are yet one, you'd better start right now, today! The gospel must go out; it must be preached and spread – it must be done fast and on a large scale.

By God's grace I have been called to preach Christ and the whole gospel of Christ to the whole world. I have devoted my entire life to him and have given myself, as his prisoner, to preach his love and saving grace. I have not been disobedient to the call God has given me. God has confirmed his call to me over the last 40 years by the fruit that has been revealed. He has confirmed that he has called me and ordained me to preach Jesus.

This is the great command of Jesus of Nazareth, the founder of our Christian faith: 'Go ye into all the world, and preach the gospel to every creature. He that believeth and is baptized shall be saved; but he that believeth not shall be damned. And these signs shall follow them that believe: In My Name shall they cast out devils; they shall speak with new tongues; they shall take up serpents; and if they drink any deadly thing it shall not hurt them; they shall lay hands on the sick, and they shall recover.'

Jesus then ascended into heaven. The disciples 'went forth, and preached everywhere, the Lord working with them, and confirming the Word with signs following' (Mark 16:15-20).

Jesus meant what he said.

The disciples heard what he said.

The disciples believed what he said.

The disciples did what he said.

And God worked with them, with signs and wonders following.

God wants to make you a soul-winner. Be obedient! Be a disciple! Hear, believe and do what the Bible says, and God is ready to do what he promised. He always confirms his Word. He is the great, unalterable changer of hearts, and his is alive. We serve and follow the living

God and his Son Jesus, who is the same yesterday, today and forever.

Be an active soul-winner, no matter who you are or what you are. Let us rejoice and work. Let us work while it is still day, until Jesus comes.

The key to this effective service and to revival, as we are seeing now, is our attitude to God. Pause for a moment and look into your heart. Ask yourself whether you are doing what you are doing for the Lord out of a passionate desire to please him. Are you doing it for him alone and his glory, or has an element of self-satisfaction crept into your so-called Christian service? If the desire to please God is not there, then your service will be meagre, cold and ineffective. It will be like polishing a car that has no engine. No amount of spit and polish will make it go! It's time to make sure your heart is right with God.

Paul said, 'I am compelled to preach Christ.' God's love changes us and drives us. We live anew as conquerors by his power. With Jesus at the controls, life can never step backward into the past. We must obey, we must go on.

THE ESSENTIAL INGREDIENT

Here is the essential ingredient of the whole gospel message: *Love*. Without it, our work for God will fall apart. With it, we become truly God's servants, and our service becomes effective for him. Paul said, 'If I have a faith that can move mountains, but have not love, I am nothing' (1 Corinthians 13:2). We are 'nothing', our service is 'nothing', everything is 'nothing' without love. We may have willingness, enthusiasm, initiative, eagerness and zeal, but without love it will come to nothing.

With God's love in me I just want to hug people, even those one would, humanly speaking, find it difficult to love. Jesus has showed me that this is the way to change the world!

The gospel is not just a set of ideas; it is God's love. In the revival people's hearts are being melted by God's love, by his signs and wonders, by the gospel message of grace. Our task is to show God's love, to make the invisible God visible to today's people. People are waiting to see this love.

In a small Lancashire town recently, people formed in queues to get into the revival meetings in the large Conservative Hall. They had to go through the club section to get to the auditorium. At the end of the meetings they passed back beside the bars, watched by the puzzled bar patrons. People who had gone into the meetings in wheelchairs left them walking, their empty wheelchairs being pushed behind them! One man who was known throughout the town, and could only walk with the aid of two walking sticks, came bouncing down the stairs into the Conservative club waving his sticks! The people at the bars were amazed: they had never seen or imagined anything like it before. It was the talk of the pubs, shops, streets, clubs and homes of that little Lancashire town for weeks afterwards. About 200 people were converted. The mission had been largely shunned by the churches of that town and was welcomed officially by only one small church, which received a flood of new converts afterwards.

I KNOW . . .

Be a Job. Job said, 'I know my redeemer liveth.' Paul said, 'I know whom I have believed and am persuaded.'

We all should know that God is with us, that he will never leave or forsake us. We should all know that the gates of hell will not prevail against the children of God. We should all know that Jesus Christ bore our sins and sicknesses on the cross of Golgotha. We should all know that God forgives all our iniquities and also heals all our diseases (Psalm 103:3). Let us be positive in our thoughts, in our speaking, in our prayer, in our faith.

If we are positive, we will not come out ashamed! Nothing can hold back the growth of the church of Jesus Christ – no slanderous tongue, no government or anything. Let us not be afraid! Let us not look upon the circumstances! Let us not look upon the greatness of the giant who is against us! We are more than conquerors through him that loved us!

The devil fights us. Some ministers and church people are hostile in some towns that I go to. In one town in South Humberside, one small church almost alone delivered literature to people's homes, inviting them to the mission meetings. The other churches didn't want to be involved. Their ministers attacked us. However, the local media gave us sympathetic coverage. Thousands flocked to the meetings, and the miracles were stunning!

As Bonnke says, the devil is 'a mouse with a microphone'! His claws were pulled out at Calvary. Scripture says he is 'a roaring lion', but he is a weak, clawless, toothless lion.

In *Pilgrim's Progress*, when Christian gets to the Castle, he has to go over a bridge, and two very fierce-looking lions are guarding it. With trepidation Christian approaches and tries to go between them. But as he looks at the great, ferocious, angry, loud-mouthed lions, he notices that they have no teeth or claws – they are defenceless! They are no more dangerous than two big toy lions!

The blood of Christ disarmed the devil. He opposes the gospel, he is the father of lies, he is the hater of blood-washed believers, he encourages every Christ-rejecter, Bible-refuser and God-despiser. But he is defeated already. 'The God of peace shall bruise Satan under you' is our promise from God. Jesus said, 'I give you power over all the power of the enemy, I give you power to walk upon serpents, I give you power to tread upon scorpions, I give you power to cast out devils.'

We don't have a small God. He has never lost a battle. He never sponsors flops, he has never failed. 'Nothing shall separate us from the love of Christ.' 'No weapon forged against us shall prosper.' The devil has been defeated but he has not yet been captured! He has lost but he has not yet capitulated!

Man is sad, disorientated in his mind. I pray for many mentally ill people, and many of them are healed. Fearful, depressed, anxious minds need God's healing, a word of encouragement, a word of peace, a listening ear. God has incalculable blessings for the distressed.

God gives us personal care and help. I like the motto of the IBM computer firm: 'We're too busy not to see you.' God is busy, and he is always glad to hear from you.

Don't be an ordinary church, don't be a sub-normal church. So many churches are dull, disinterested, indifferent. We need fiery, burning, abnormal, Christ-centred, Spirit-filled, born-again disciples. The heart of revival is making Jesus Lord. Together God's people can make a difference. God is raising up people and ministries of joy. The power of divine joy is elevating, refreshing. People need to be uplifted; the world is waiting to see the coming of the sons of God in their power. It has begun! Multitudes are being astonished in our great campaigns nationwide. Jesus is front-page news! The gospel is shocking the humanists with its deep impact on millions. In an unquestionable way God is unveiling his beauty and his Divine heart to thousands.

A WIND OF CONVICTION

A deep wind of conviction is blowing. Hurts are being healed, tears are being wiped away, past failures are vanishing, wrongs are being righted through the Divine river of God's truth touching so many hearts.

When you are totally given up to him, his lordship covers your body, your thoughts, your tongue, your temper, your moods, your behaviour, your life-plans, your spare time, your wallet, your recreation and your church life. You are set free to serve God.

Many church leaders stand aloof from the revival. Many are asking God to send revival, but it has already come! The new emphasis is to be filled with the Holy Ghost and to go and evangelize in his power. The old emphasis on restoration, on the church, on blessing believers continuously and forgetting Britain's unsaved people must come to an end – it's a dead end! We must return to the cross, to Holy Ghost power, to the passion for souls!

With the vigorous preaching of the gospel, thousands in the UK are finding hope! We need to be more daring. In so many places the Christians are asleep in their house meetings, in their large New Life churches, in their celebrations, in their Bible weeks and camps, in their nice cosy fellowships!

Think of the glorious daring of those early apostles! Little wonder that the world called them mad! Paul was satisfied with nothing less than taking the gospel to the world, including the capital, Rome. These men and women of the past have handed on the torch to us. We too must have the same vision, the same zeal, the same willingness to sacrifice. We must dare to believe God for even greater things in the years ahead.

Our command comes from the Lord Jesus Christ: 'Ye shall receive power, after that the Holy Ghost is come upon you: and ye shall be witnesses unto me both in Jerusalem, and in all Judea, and in Samaria, and unto the uttermost part of the earth.' This command is recorded in Scripture at least five times in one form or another. Some scholars say that Jesus repeated the command over and over again. Jesus said to the demon-possessed man of Gadara, 'Go home to thy friends, and tell them of the great things the Lord hath done for thee.'

DESPERATE PEOPLE

We are experiencing the 'desperateness of evangelism', what someone called 'the luxury of winning souls'. But it is more than a luxury if it is to count for anything. Krummacher, the great German preacher, wrote, 'I look upon every man's soul as a castle which I must storm and win for Christ.' We need to be desperate people: 'The kingdom of heaven suffereth violence, and the violent take it' (Matthew 11:12). Earnest, urgent, desperate people win the lost. Dr James Denney said, 'The Kingdom of God is not for the well meaning, it is for the desperate.' Be desperate to turn our nation back.

We must obey what Jesus said: 'Go, and do . . .' (Luke 10:37); 'Go, and show . . .' (Luke 5:14); 'Go out quickly into the streets and lanes . . .' (Luke 14:21); 'Go out into the highways and hedges . . .' (Luke 14:23); 'Go . . . into

the vineyard . . .' (Matthew 20:4, 7); 'Go into the village
. . .' (Matthew 21:2); 'Go into the city . . .' (Matthew
26:18); 'Go into the next town . . .' (Mark 1:38); 'Go . . .
to the lost sheep . . .' (Matthew 10:6); 'Go . . . and preach
the kingdom of God . . .' (Luke 9:60); 'Go . . . into all the
world . . .' (Mark 16:15).

And with his commands ringing in their ears, Jesus'
disciples set out not only to reach the world, but also to
turn it upside down in their generation (Acts 17:6). They
suffered hardship, persecution, beatings and death. But
they said, 'We cannot but speak the things which we
have seen and heard' (Acts 4:20).

We are a people under authority. We are under
command. Our Commander in Chief says, 'Go!' We
must obey. We must go and witness.

Billy Graham said recently, 'Time after time in church
history the message has been blunted and watered down
and diluted. But time after time the church has recovered
its message and has continued to spread the gospel, and
the church has continued to grow.'

Let us not give in to our generation's permissiveness,
hardness, weakness, moral waverings, spiritual lightness, carnalities and lack of love. Let us recover the
message, the power, the confidence, the miraculous
anointing, and win the whole land for King Jesus.

God is mightily at work on every continent. The
headlines in our newspapers tell us of all the bad things
that are happening, but there is a mighty spiritual
movement in many countries throughout the world.

The early apostles had no doubt about what they
were to preach: 'Neither is there salvation in any other:
for there is no other name under heaven given among
men, whereby we must be saved' (Acts 4:12). It was
Jesus that they preached.

The message that Christians have always proclaimed is the cross, the resurrection, the necessity of repentance and faith and the call to discipleship.

I've preached this message all over the UK and all over the world. And I have found that the human heart is the same the world over. The gospel is the answer to the longing and the tears and the guilt of every human heart. I've seen people everywhere respond in the same way to the gospel.

I am seeing revival in Britain today – in small villages in the Shetland Isles, among the wild Bikers who are coming to Christ in droves, among hundreds of Gipsies, among black and white, in the toughest working-class areas. God is melting, breaking, cleansing and changing thousands of lives!

God calls us to the whole of our world. The world that our Lord was talking about includes the geographical world. But it also includes the psychological world and the sociological world. It includes the worlds of school and business and government and labour. Be a witness to Christ wherever you go.

The world is hungry and waiting. I find an openness to the gospel today on a scale I've not known in my many years of evangelism: 'The fields . . . are white already to harvest' (John 4:35). But harvest time is always brief. Jesus warned, 'The night cometh, when no man can work' (John 9:4). Be desperate, give it all, throw everything on Christ.

THE SPIRIT'S POWER

Some years ago there was a picture in a magazine showing a straw which had penetrated a pole during a tornado. I asked myself, 'How could such a fragile straw penetrate a pole?' It was because the power of the wind blowing it was so tremendous.

Christ has promised us power. God's spiritual energy reserves never run out. Jesus said, 'Ye shall receive power, after that the Holy Ghost is come upon you' (Acts 1:8). Our power comes from the Holy Spirit.

The Holy Spirit prepares hearts (Proverbs 16:1); the Spirit guides us (John 16:13); the Spirit gives us boldness (Acts 4:31); the Spirit has given us the Word of God (2 Peter 1:21); the Spirit gives us wisdom (1 Corinthians 12:8); the Spirit alone can bring conviction (John 16:8) and faith (1 Corinthians 12:9). Therefore we are dependent on him. Our mission will never be accomplished by organizations or by methods alone. It will be accomplished by the power of the Holy Spirit working through us.

Jesus said, 'If any will come after Me, let him deny himself, and take up his cross daily, and follow Me' (Luke 9:23). In the New Testament the word 'Christian' is used only three times – in Acts 11:26, Acts 26:28 and 1 Peter 4:16. And in each of these instances it is associated with suffering, and persecution is in the background. To serve Christ is costly. Jesus said, 'Count the cost' (Luke 14:28).

From a small dedication or reconsecration, a small life, a little talent, a timid person, an ungifted one, a has-been, God can take you up and use you today, and from now on.

On his 59th birthday David Livingstone wrote, 'My Jesus, my King, my life, my All; I again dedicate my whole self to Thee.' And that is what I am asking you to do: to surrender your life totally and completely to Christ. With the songwriter, say with all your heart, 'I surrender all.' No terms except unconditional and immediate surrender can be accepted. That is what Christ demands.

And Paul wrote, 'Do not surrender the members of your personality as instruments of unrighteousness to sin, but rather surrender yourselves fully to God, as those who are alive from the dead' (Romans 6:13).

God uses our enthusiasm, persistence, stickability, faith, love, grit, risk and prayer!

A young man went west some years ago and found himself in California with no more than a few dollars in his pocket. He went to a bank. 'I want to buy a garage,' he said. 'Will you lend me some money?'

'Sorry,' said the manager. 'If you've no security, we can do nothing for you.' So the door slammed in his face. What did he do? What would you have done? Given up?

Well, he got a job at the smallest garage in Los Angeles. He worked hard. In five years, what had been the smallest became the biggest garage thereabouts.

Then he went again to see the bank manager, and got an advance of 150,000 dollars. Today, he's behind one of the biggest motor services in the United States.

See the idea? One door shuts. OK. Accept the challenge. Open another!

Start like a little seed, bury yourself in God, and by his hand it will grow into a mighty work and blessing for him.

SURRENDER

Be willing to surrender again to him – surrender your spirit to Christ for fulfilment. Surrender your body to Christ for dominion. Surrender your will to Christ for occupation. Surrender your mind to Christ for mastery.

Surrender your conscience to Christ for control. Surrender your mobility to Christ for purity. Surrender your time to Christ for lordship. Surrender your talents to Christ for leadership. Surrender your relationships to Christ for his glory. Surrender your destiny to Christ for eternal life.

Jesus is the maker of men. He said, 'Follow Me, and I will make you fishers of men' (Matthew 4:19). He wants to remake us, remould us, rehabilitate us and revitalize us.

Paul said, 'For me to life in Christ.' Dr Sangster said, 'He wants to be King of your life, not president. A King rules for life, but a president only for a short stay.'

Wesley was settled down in a nice curacy, but God shook him up, to ride out and save England. Carey mended boots in his Northampton cobbler's shop, but God spoke to him and sent him to India. Livingstone could have had an easy life as a doctor in Scotland, but God breathed on him, and so Africa was opened to Christ. Jackie Pullinger was rejected by the official missionary societies, but she still went, and she has turned Hong Kong upside down. The dying George Jefferies laid hands on a young Bible student named Reinhardt Bonnke, and he is reaching whole nations for King Jesus in the Third World today!

Nearly 200 years ago there were two Scottish brothers named John and David Livingstone. John had set his mind on making money and becoming wealthy, and he did. But in an old *Encyclopaedia Britannica*, John Livingstone is simply listed as 'the brother of David Livingstone'.

And who was David Livingstone? While John had dedicated himself to making money, David had knelt down and prayed. In surrendering himself to Christ, he resolved, 'I will place no value on anything I have or possess unless it is in relationship to the Kingdom of God.' The inscription over his burial place in Westminster Abbey reads, 'For thirty years his life was spent in the unwearied effort to evangelize.'

GOING SOMEWHERE

Some years ago someone was looking at Sir Frank Salisbury's superb painting of the great evangelist John Wesley. Greatly moved by the portrait, the person said, 'It's a wonderful face. It's the face of a man who is going somewhere.' Christ offers you somewhere to go, someone to love, something to do.

Go with the cross, go with God, go in his guidance, go in his direction, go for lost souls. Kneel at the cross. Give yourself to spread its message.

Join me in saying, 'As best as I know how, I want to surrender all to the Lord Jesus Christ. I want to be a new man or woman. I surrender all. I want to be Christ's ambassador. I want to serve him. I want to be his witness.'

DOUBTERS

The doubters are saying, 'It cannot be a genuine revival!' Some Christians, shut up in their nice little churches, or molly-coddled in their giant congregations, are missing the revival.

In the great 18th-century revival, when Wesley, Whitfield, John Brand and others moved around sharing God's Word, many called them 'innovators' or opportunists. People are saying similar things about today's revival. Even some who have prayed for it for so long, now deny it when it has come.

The Christians of the early church were always expecting and experiencing the unusual. Britain's church of the 20th century is expected to be drab, staid, formal, law-abiding and respectable! But in Acts there were sensational jail-breaks, sensational miracles, sensational happenings, sensational conversions, sensational deliverances! This is what is happening today. In the revival we are again seeing the supernatural power of God.

We need to be touched by the presence of God. It is on God's heart to touch this nation. That is why we are so highly favoured at this time of blessing.

We are bringing Good News for a sad age. As I walk through the door in so many revival meetings, it is there before I open my mouth to preach – the power of Almighty God! The love of God, the presence of God, the holiness of God is there. Soon people are converted by wave after wave of the Holy Spirit. God keeps His Word.

The little child said with glee and bright open eyes, 'My Dad promised me a skate board!' He hasn't got it yet, it hasn't arrived yet, he doesn't know where it is, he hasn't seen it yet, he has never tried it, he has never felt it beneath him as he propels himself along. It's all a promise. But, to the little boy, it's almost a reality, and the promise means as much as when he actually has it, because he trusts his father.

God wants to give millions the kiss of forgiveness. We are sons of the living God by faith and a changed heart. We are touching the hem of revival. Strange, unique things are taking place. Miracles are on the front pages of the newspapers, conversions are plentiful, new churches are being planted. There is a new devotion to God's purposes.

Big men are falling on their knees in repentance. Holiness is sweeping many parts of the land. The presence of God is so heavy that we cannot close the meetings and go home till after midnight in most places. One man, unused to this type of conviction, although a regular churchgoer, commented, 'I'm frightened to stay here any longer – I must go home!' When he got home he was still disturbed, and he had to return to the meeting to kneel and pray in repentance, and later he apologized to the preacher.

In another church, although there were many conversions and healings, many people grumbled. They complained that I did not pray long enough for the sick. But with 100 or more to pray for, the prayers must be brief, or we would be there all night!

Great blessing often brings out the critics, and revival is always opposed. Revival is a time of defeat for the enemy. An epidemic of revival has begun, resulting in mass conversions. God is at work in an awesome way. The people of our day are crying, 'Nothing like this has ever been seen in our land' (Matthew 9:33).

He is the God of immense power. He is the God of the immeasurable. The release of Divine power leaves us amazed again and again. God is making himself known to our world. We are being reinstated into the power of the Lord. God is raising up miraculously the casualties of 20th-century life. God is not disappointing us. All heaven is upon our side. The gospel is the 'power of God unto salvation'.

He is leading us into dangerous living, victorious living. The fire has come. God is yielding to us magnificent rewards. We are living in the gospel power, seeing gloriously changed lives.

Revival is in the air – we are offering a hand of love

to the spiritually starving people, working great acts of power in his name and by his Word.

UNCOMPROMISING

Malcolm Muggeridge wrote, 'The world is in idiot despair . . . depraved and desolate . . . but be steadfast, unmoveable in a distintegrating world, and in the midst of the breakdown of the church . . . let us see Christ.'

God wants to let you loose on the unsuspecting population. Are you evangelizing your town? Or are you inward looking? Backslidden Britain is being confronted by a growing band of Christians who have come from the presence of God, with a clear, uncompromising message. They know God intimately and declare his Word with holy authority, because they live before him. God only backs uncompromising prophets.

Some hermits lived in a little monastery, shut away from the world. One day someone asked them through a slit in the wall, 'Are you dead?' They replied, 'We are dead to the world.' No one will have any effect on the world like that! We must come from behind closed doors and lighten the world. They can only see God and feel his presence through us!

Jesus did not hide away from the crowds. He sat with publicans, talked to prostitutes, challenged lawyers. He earned the title, 'friend of publicans and sinners'. He was untouched by man's sin, and yet he was amongst man.

RISING TO THE CHALLENGE

Many churches and Christians are living at an abnormal level. But suddenly many other believers are being moved from their state of lethargy, laziness and sleepiness into a new awareness of the Spirit. We are beginning to see everything as we never saw it before. From a diet of back-biting, failure, division, weak fellowship and constant criticism, God is sweeping and rousing some people to new peaks of challenge. The saints are being swept off their feet, they are losing their sense of proportion, they are getting the burden of God on them. When God takes the stage, anything can happen. He is the God of holiness, the unpredictable One, the God of surprises.

Many are rising to his challenge of spiritual elevation. Ministers who once wilted at the prospect of early morning prayer meetings, of the prodding to sacrificial living, who quailed before the thought of the influx of great numbers of converts and untaught Christians, and endlessly long meetings, are now having a new personal walk with God. They are rising to the Christ-like character, and to a new relationship with God.

The secret, then, lies in this intimacy with Christ. In one place where many were gathering at 5 a.m. prayer meetings to seek God's face, tremendous revival was flowing in. When they prayed all day, one cynic commented, 'They have got nothing better to do! The reply came back, 'Is there anything better to do?'

FIND YOUR NICHE

God is calling many people into the harvest field. Many have caught fire late in life. Quite rightly, our churches today emphasize the great potential of young people, but this should not mean overlooking the potential of old people. The prophet Joel foresaw the day when 'Your old men will dream dreams' (Joel 2:28).

There are many options open to the Christian worker who has retired from a secular occupation but is still hale and hearty. I know a retired doctor who offers his services as a locum overseas to relieve the pressure in a missionary hospital. There are plenty of retired businessmen who have accepted ordination to the ministry or have become lay pastors.

There are, of course, many less arduous jobs in the local church which are ideal for retired people, such as the regular visiting of elderly and shut-in folk, administrative tasks, counselling, baby-sitting, prison visiting and suchlike.

Many lose their glow and joy and need reviving again. The middle years are often the greatest threat to our keenness as Christians. Many of us have to ask wistfully with the poet:

> *Where is the blessedness I knew*
> *When first I saw the Lord?*
> *Where is the soul-refreshing view*
> *Of Jesus and His Word?*

To serve God where he wants us to serve him is a delight beyond all comparison. Old or young, we must all find our niche. And the most important job is to win others to Christ. God is calling us to play our part.

We must set the pace. In many towns, the ministers have been so cautious and slow for generations that revival is beginning amongst the lowliest, humblest of believers, in the grass roots, and the pastors and leaders are following later! We must bear fruit. We must stick at it, like the lady whose house was being repossessed in the dreadful recession of the late 1980s. She got some extra-strong glue and glued herself to the stairs of her home!

When the bailiffs came they could not move her and gave up! She won her home back through this. As the newspapers put it, quoting her, 'I'm going to stick it out!'

GIVE GOD THE GLORY

Although a Christian faces many temptations, one of the greatest is the temptation to take to oneself credit that is due only to God. Difficult though it may be for us to understand, it is a firm scriptural principle that God will not share his glory with anyone else. God says, 'For my own sake . . . I do this. How can I let myself be defamed? I will not yield my glory to another' (Isaiah 48:11). Our attitude must always be to give the Lord all the glory. A victory is only complete, a healing is only finalized when we give God the sole praise.

6

NATION AND CHURCH

In Isaiah chapter 1, God speaks through the prophet about Israel's deteriorating attitude towards their Lord. What was wrong? 'I reared up children and brought them up, but they have rebelled against me' (Isaiah 1:2). God had taken the first step in choosing a people for himself; it is always he who takes the initiative. He called Abraham and brought into being a nation from his descendants. But God's own people turned away from him, and God had to say to them: 'The ox knows his master, the donkey his owner's manger, but Israel does not know, my people do not understand' (Isaiah 1:3).

Israel had drifted so far that they no longer knew where they belonged. This could be applied to Christians in Europe today, in 'post-Christian Europe' as some would call it. Salvation has been offered to us through Jesus Christ. Heaven's gates have been flung wide open so that we can have fellowship with our Father. But we need to ask whether we too have drifted away. Are we so busy with our daily life that we have forgotten our first love?

In his outstanding book, *Money and Power*, Jacques Ellul examines our attitudes towards money. Solomon and Job were blessed by God and became very rich, but Jesus described money as 'mammon', a powerful idol to which many have sold their souls. Ellul argues that money is good or bad depending on the place it has in our relationship with God. It can be a blessing, or it can be a curse.

God shows his amazing love when he refers to a sinful nation as 'children' and 'my people' (Isaiah 1:2-3). They are 'children given to corruption' (verse 4), but still they remain as children, and he wants them back.

Even when we turn away from our Father, he calls us back. Isaiah explained that God's judgement of the Israelites was lovingly intended to help them to turn back to him. 'Why should you be beaten any more? Why do you persist in rebellion?' (verse 5). The obstacles are of our own making; they are not in the Father's heart.

KEEPING UP APPEARANCES?

The people in Isaiah's day went to the temple with their sacrifices, but their songs and prayers were no more than a religious routine. And God said through Isaiah: 'Your New Moon festivals and your appointed feasts my soul hates' (Isaiah 1:14). The festivals had become people-centred gatherings; they were no longer for God.

This should make us ask questions about our own churchgoing. Are we seeking the Lord and enjoying our relationship with him, or are we just keeping up our religious appearances?

God is always calling his people back. 'Come now, let us reason together,' says the Lord. 'Though your sins are like scarlet, they shall be as white as the snow; though they are red as crimson, they shall be like wool' (Isaiah 1:18). Revival would have broken out if this message had been acted upon, and the promise is still true for us today. The Lord restores our relationship with him when we turn away from our sin and look to him in renewed obedience.

Isaiah took the whole of chapter 1 to make Israel aware of their spiritual condition. Then in chapter 2 he told them how God was eager to call them back to himself: 'In the last days the mountain of the Lord's temple will be established as chief among the mountains . . . Many peoples will come and say, "Come, let us go up to the mountain of the Lord, to the house of the God of Jacob" ' (Isaiah 2:2).

God is purging and refining, bringing a resplendent people to the fore. They are small in number but ever growing, a people who look for the triumph of the Kingdom. They are longing for better things, keeping to the heavenly vision, storming the ramparts of heaven, evangelizing the lost, going with the flaming evangel, emblazoning his name and fame in a million hearts.

The challenge rings in our ears: build a new relationship with God. Isaiah prepares the people for the wonderful things that God is going to do in days to come. Just like someone who is getting ready for a wedding, we are to be prepared for all that God has in store for us.

Our theory is recovering its original meaning – that is, knowing about God. Our hearts hunger for God and are satisfied with 'the surpassing greatness of knowing Christ Jesus my Lord, for whose sake I have lost all things' (Philippians 3:8).

God has given us everything we need to build up our relationship with him. Bible reading and meditation inspire our hearts to pray according to God's Word. The Holy Spirit directs us as we listen to his promptings.

Fellowship with other Christians should stimulate us and correct us in our walk with the Lord. God honours those who seek him, who are hungry for reality and refuse to be satisfied by second-rate spirituality.

God is raising up a new breed of believers who have been washed in Jesus' blood and filled with the Holy Spirit. They are paying the price, seeking revival, walking full of life, defeating and ousting the devil, exercising spiritual gifts, living in the supernatural, exuding peace, abiding in the Scriptures and partaking of God's divine nature.

The history of the British nation can be summed up as follows:

> from bondage to spiritual faith,
> from faith to great courage,
> from courage to liberty,
> from liberty to abundance,
> from abundance to apathy,
> from apathy to dependency,
> from dependency to bondage once again ...

It is indeed time for spiritual faith to start again.

Six students wanted to go out into the bay to fish. The wise old fisherman warned them of sudden storms. 'Oh, we'll be okay. Don't worry.' They offered him extra money, heedless of his warnings. He took them out. They had not been fishing for long, when suddenly a great storm was immediately ahead. The old fisherman warned them, 'We'd better get back.' He was really worried. The young fellows boasted, 'Oh, we'll be okay. We've got plenty of time. Let's fish a bit more.' The old sailor's face got more grave. He remonstrated, 'We must get back!' They sighed, 'There's no real danger. We'll be all right.' Then, turning the boat around towards the harbour, the man of the sea called out, 'Yes, you're too ignorant to be afraid!'

People today are too ignorant to be afraid. They do not fear God. They are too ignorant, too dark, too unknowing of the dangers and the perils. God's people are not aware of the perils of unjudged sin, of being ignorant of the Almighty's judgements. The church has failed to tell the people what sin is!

The modern British church has become a laughing matter. It is the butt of TV, radio and press jokes! But the miracles which are taking place in the present revival are making the media and the world take notice.

The cross of Jesus is the only weapon which can defeat the devil, but God's people are just not using it. They are too concerned about protecting themselves about preserving the status quo. The supernatural is missing in many churches, and Christians have as many idols as other religions. Without the real Jesus, without the power of the blood-covered cross, we have nothing to offer the world. We must lift up the bleeding form of Jesus as the ultimatum to the devil, as the only answer to mans' sin and dilemma. Without miracles we are a failure. I urge you to let God loose in you!

7

THE CROSS AND THE BLOOD

The central theme of the present revival is the cross of Jesus Christ. On that cross his sinless soul soaked up the black ocean of mankind's sin. The sacred soul of Jesus actually became sin for us. The cancellation of our sin is written in Christ's blood. He paid the dowry in blood and agony. He suffered violence, pain, humiliation and degradation on the cross. Isaiah wrote, 'The Lord laid on him the iniquity of us all.'

Through the cross of Jesus countless men and women can pass from a life of sin to a life of purity, from the slavery of fear into the freedom of total deliverance. Even the desire to sin as well as the habit of sinning can be broken. Like a binding chain, it can be snapped. Charles Wesley wrote in one of his famous hymns:

> *My chains fell off, my heart was free,*
> *I rose, went forth, and followed thee.*

All men can enjoy this great salvation. There is no restriction because of age, sex, nationality, status, learning, intelligence or colour. Any and all may come:

> *There's room at the Cross for you,*
> *Though millions have come,*
> *There's still room for one,*
> *Yes, there's room at the Cross for you.*

Faith is the switch which connects us human beings into the pardoning flow of God. Salvation is not by penance, by suffering, by priests or by evangelists. We cannot merit it by special prayers, works or money. It's faith that connects us up to the Divine dynamo of Calvary. Faith makes the blood of Christ work for us. 'For by grace are ye saved through faith; and that not of yourselves: it is the gift of God. Not of works, lest any man should boast' (Ephesians 2:8-9).

A doctor in Glasgow had to treat two young mothers suffering from the same complaint. There was no known cure for this illness at the time, and everyone concerned was worried. Browsing through the latest medical journal, he suddenly sat up with a thrill. In America, a scientist had made a breakthrough which concerned this very condition. The doctor went to the phone immediately, and after some expensive phone calls, he arranged for the drug to be flown over to Prestwick. Knowing how urgent the situation was, he met the plane, and within two or three hours he visited both his patients with the good news, leaving careful and detailed instructions of the dosage to be taken.

Within three weeks one lady was up and making splendid progress. The other died. This puzzled the doctor so much that a few days after the funeral, he called on the broken-hearted widower. The doctor explained his puzzlement to the husband. The man replied: 'Doctor, I can quite easily give you the answer.' With tears the young man said: 'That first night, I tried my utmost to get my wife to take the medicine. She said she had suffered enough, and simply flushed it all down the toilet.'

It was the right medicine to do the job. It was brought by a caring doctor at considerable personal cost. It was within her grasp and it was free. Could anyone blame the doctor for what happened? The only person anyone could blame was the one who refused the offer.

What Jesus has to offer will meet our need. It is within our grasp and it is free. Only fools reject it!

The miracle power of Calvary has not deteriorated in value or effect. Many have watered down the message, but the blood of Jesus has eternal validity. We see our world drowning in disillusionment, drifting in the depths of despair. His cross outlives, outlasts and outshines all other powers. Calvary saw the release of miracle power that produces spectacular scenes in our modern-day missions. As faith is proclaimed and manifested, we are seeing revival and the victory of God's Word in thousands of hearts.

MISSION ACCOMPLISHED

The Saviour did not merely come to show others how to live on earth. He came to die and make it possible for us to live eternally in heaven. He came to create a corridor through which his creation could come back to God.

During the Second World War, 'Mission accomplished' was the message sent back by Morse code to HQ by a lone soldier, as he lay dying. He had been sent to blast the concrete defences around a military establishment. Similarly, Christ has cracked the concrete crust of sin's brutal barrier, and now, as the hymnwriter has put it: 'There's a way back to God from the dark paths of sin'. Satan's defences are demolished. He thought he could bring Christ down into his domain of death, only to find that he could not kill the Christ. His every attempt had failed. On the cross Jesus shouted aloud: 'It is finished!' His mission was accomplished, completed and totally fulfilled. He did not say, 'I am finished' but 'It is finished'.

What Jesus did for us on the cross will never need to be repeated. As Harold Horton put it, 'The one transaction in Golgotha's holy market place is enough now and forever.' Jesus paid the debt, bridged the gap, settled the old accounts, cleared our past and redeemed us by his own blood.

All the blessings of salvation – grace, our inheritance in Christ, power, joy, marvels and wonders of faith – are through the precious blood of Christ, through the finished work of the cross.

The cross is:

an advocate which pleads our cause
an advertisement announcing God's love for us
a bank in which the riches of God's grace are stored
a canopy under which we find protection from God's wrath
a drawing-board on which God drew the plan of salvation
an exhibition of a true character of compassion
a finger pointing the way to heaven
a goal on which Jesus set his sights to save us all
a ladder from the depths of sin into the arms of Jesus
a magnet which draws us to salvation
an oasis where thirsty souls can come and find refreshment
a pulpit from which the gospel of free grace is preached
a refuge to which we may come and find safety from the enemy
a spotlight focusing on the substitutionary work of Calvary
a tree of life to all who believe.

It has been said that a blood covenant made between two kings in the Middle East was the most binding of all known covenants. The traditional ceremony was quite an occasion. The date and place was mutually agreed by the regal participants. In some cases the event was an illustrious occasion with ample pomp, colour, feasting and happiness. Sometimes it would last for several days. When the vital moment arrived, the two kings would emerge from their tents, each with a sharp knife in his hand. After bowing to the ground, they would rise and stand facing each other. Each of them would cut a vein in his wrist. Then putting their wrists together, they would hold them in such a way that the blood of the two men would mingle, the significance being that each could say, 'I have some of your blood in me and you have some of my blood in you.' This meant that they were now 'blood brothers'. The significance behind all this was that, in the event of either of them being in any kind of difficulty, or if either was being attacked by an enemy, they could count on the other coming to their assistance with all his resources. They were bound by the blood covenant they had made to stand by, defend or assist one another. The resources of their blood brother were now fully available in any time of need. It was an irreversible covenant, for they could never take the other's blood out of their body. Therefore it was an everlasting, unchangeable, irrevocable covenant.

What a glorious picture of the New Covenant sealed in the blood of Jesus. It was the King of Kings who held out his wrists to bring forth his precious blood in order to make this eternal, unchangeable and irreversible

New Covenant. The Saviour was fully aware of all the implications involved in what he was doing when he spoke these inspired words: 'This cup is the New Covenant in My blood, which is shed for you' (Luke 22:20).

Here, in a few words, are the benefits of the New Covenant into which any man of any nation can enter, provided they will repent of their sins and believe in their heart that God raised Jesus from the dead:

(1) Total forgiveness of every sin.
(2) Escape from divine judgement in an eternal hell.
(3) The assurance of divine life coming into our soul.
(4) When we receive this eternal life we are born again.
(5) The promise that the Holy Spirit will come in and guide us, protect us, and teach us.
(6) Our names will be written in the book of life, making our eternal destiny in heaven secure.
(7) We become part of the family of God.

On our part, we must be gladly willing to repent of our sins and to accept Jesus as the Lord of our lives. In simple language, this means doing his will and fulfilling his purposes in our daily living. It also means that all our resources and talents are available to him at any time.

The miracle power of the sacrifice of Calvary touches our hearts, our homes, our lives, our worship. Today thousands are being miraculously saved and healed through the power of Jesus' cross.

As Charles Spurgeon said, 'Christ died for me. That is the root of every satisfaction I have.' Our peace is through the cross. The cross was in the heart of God aeons before it stood starkly on the crest of the hill of Calvary. 'The Lamb was slain from the foundation of the world' (Revelation 13: 8). And it will be in the heart of God when time shall be no more.

PROPHECY

It was prophesied that Jesus Christ would suffer for us:

'They shall smite the Judge of Israel with a rod upon the cheek' (Micah 5:1).
'They smote him with the palms of their hands' (Matthew 26:67).

'I hid not my face from spitting' (Isaiah 50:6).
'They did spit in his face' (Matthew 26:67).

'I gave my back to the smiters' (Isaiah 50:6).
'Then Pilate took Jesus and scourged him' (John 19:1).

'Many were astonished at thee; his visage was so marred more than any man' (Isaiah 52:14).
'They buffeted him' (Matthew 26:67); 'They struck him on the face' (Luke 22:64).

'As a sheep before her shearers is dumb, so he openeth not his mouth' (Isaiah 53:7).
'He answered nothing . . . He answered him to never a word, insomuch that the governor marvelled greatly' (Matthew 27:12,14).

What is the cross? Ask a carpenter. 'It is only two lengths of timber,' he will tell you. 'A couple of beams.' What is the cross? Ask a botanist. 'It is wood,' he will inform you, 'from the trunk of an oak, cedar, sycamore, or the like.' What is the cross? Ask a jurist. 'It is an instrument of capital punishment,' he will reply, 'now happily discarded by our modern, more civilized, humanitarian society.' What is the cross? Ask a Christian. 'It is the most wonderful thing in the world,' he will answer, 'for there will come a day when everything else that one possesses will have to be left behind, and the cross will then, as now, be the sole bridge from time to eternity, from earth to heaven. It is life's supreme prize.'

Martin Luther was right when he said: 'The true cross of Christendom is that cross of Christ which is divided throughout the whole world, not of particles of wood, but that cross which comes to each as his own portion of life.'

The cross, as I have said, is no cushioned gibbet. 'No man,' wrote Samuel Rutherford, 'hath a velvet cross, but the cross is made of that which God will have it.' 'When Christ calls a man,' declared Dietrich Bonhoeffer, hanged in a Nazi concentration camp, 'he bids him come and die.'

Ian McPherson told of a wealthy American and his wife who went to Oberammergau in Bavaria to see the Passion Play. At the time the famous Anton Lang was the Christus. After a performance at which they were present, he placed the cross he was carrying against a wall on the stage. The American had a high-powered camera and, seeing Lang laying the cross down, he thought it would be a capital idea to have a photograph taken of himself bearing it. Handing the camera to his wife, he climbed on to the stage and went over to where the cross was lying and tried to pick it up. The cross was too heavy for him to carry. Approaching Lang, he remarked: 'I did not know that the cross was so heavy.' Drawing himself up to his full stature, the actor replied with dignity: 'Sir, if I did not feel the weight of his cross, I could not play his part!'

The full weight of his cross is coming to bear on this generation in the new revival. The blazing figure on the central cross is gripping thousands across Britain today. The 1990s is the hour of revival. The cross is returning to its own again. 'When Christ had called the people unto him, with the disciples also, he said unto them, 'Whosoever will come after Me, let him deny himself, and take up his cross, and follow Me' (Mark 8:34).

Paul said, 'I die in Christ . . .' There must be surrender and sacrifice if we are to feel and know the power of Calvary in our ministries, message, witnessing, church-life and meetings. Few are willing to pay the price.

B. D. Johns wrote, 'He who has been on the Cross for us, has promised to be under the Cross with us.' And he is able to lift not only the cross, but us with it and on it by his superlative supporting power. Thus thousands are being changed, uplifted and radiantly transformed by the proclaiming of the finished work of Calvary in this magnificent new revival!

FAITH, NOT WORKS

Nothing less than the death of God's own Son could cancel the charges nailed over the door of my life. But how do I receive this credit note which is of eternal value? 'The whole thing, then, is a matter of faith on man's part and generosity on God's . . . Now this counting of faith for righteousness was not recorded simply for Abraham's credit, but as a divine principle which should apply to us as well' (Romans 4:16-23, J. B. Phillips).

Abrahams believed God's promise, and that was credited to him. The same credit is available to us, by using the same simple faith as did Abraham. The prison superintendent in Philippi asked Paul: 'What must I do to be saved?' The straightforward reply was: 'Believe on the Lord Jesus Christ and thou shalt be saved' (Acts 16:30-31).

Martin Luther had his eyes opened to this great fact while going up some steps in Rome on his knees. The Holy Spirit shone into his soul like a beam of light from heaven, as he grasped this verse of Scripture: 'The just shall live by faith' (Romans 1:17). In that moment he sprang to his feet, grasping the implication of this basic truth. Forgiveness is not by works, penance or prayers. It is by wholly trusting in the finished work of Jesus on the cross. Now I am credited with this pardon which cancels the debt I could never pay. How thrilling it is to grasp this fact! God took the initiative. Paul puts it like this: 'God commendeth his love towards us, in that while we were yet sinners, Christ died for us' (Romans 5:8).

A famous French pop star once walked the streets of Paris on her knees, with sharp stones tied round her legs. She was bleeding and in great pain. Asked the reason for this strange behaviour, the star said, 'That I might find peace with God.' She did not know that 'The just suffered for the unjust, the righteous one [Christ] suffered for the unrighteous.' 'Neither by the blood of bulls and goats . . . but by his own blood he entered in . . . having obtained eternal redemption for us . . . How much more shall the blood of Christ . . . purge your conscience from dead works.'

The Good News is that not only did Jesus Christ die for us, but he also rose again, vanquishing death. He lives today in the power of endless life, to provide immortality to those who will trust him and entrust their lives to his power. These things are not theories, but facts; they are not opinions, but realities.

George Fox, the great Quaker evangelist, used to cry, 'Tell them about the Lamb of God till you can tell them no more.' The Lamb of God, the precious Son of God, our Lord Jesus Christ had to sprinkle his blood so that we could be forgiven by God and reconciled to God. The old hymn, which has had a revival in recent days, goes:

> *What can wash away my sin?*
> *Nothing but the Blood of Jesus.*
> *What can make me whole again?*
> *Nothing but the Blood of Jesus.*
>
> *O precious is the flow*
> *That washes white as snow.*
> *No other fount I know,*
> *Nothing but the Blood of Jesus.*

It is the blood that gives your body life. If you go to the doctor's and there is something wrong with your blood, then there is disease in your body. I was recently checked over by a doctor, and he said, 'Your cholesterol is low, the sugar in your body is low. Your blood is A1. You are fit and you will live to be 100!' Well, that's in God's hands, isn't it? But if the blood is good, it is a healthy sign.

The atonement is the central doctrine of the Christian faith: 'And he is the propitiation for our sins: and not for ours only, but also for the sins of the whole world' (1 John 2:2).

Sin is serious, sin is strong, sin is hostility to God, independence of God, human defiance of God. Gipsy Smith used to say, 'Sin is something very evil, when it took the red, bleeding hands of Jesus on the cross to deal with it.' How true. Scripture tells us, 'The Lord laid on him the iniquity of us all.' Karl Barth said, 'God's own heart suffered on the cross.' Bonhoeffer declared, 'Only the suffering God can save us.' John Stott writes, 'No doctrine is truly Christian which is not centred on the cross.' Dr Michael Green says, 'The cross is the core of the gospel.'

VICTORY

A few years ago the *Daily Mail* reported an amusing incident in London. A burglar was getting away from a house with a bag of loot. An overweight policeman gave chase, but the thief was getting away, being young and agile. However, the policeman was a good mimicker of animal noises. In the dark he barked and threw his voice like a great, baying Doberman! Again and again the snarl and vicious growl snapped just behind the running thief. He finally threw down his bag and gave himself up, and the constable made a sharp arrest. But there was no vicious dog, only a bark!

Similarly, the devil barks loudly, but he has no power to harm us. The devil has been beaten already by Jesus. The devil is powerless against the believer who is living under, believing in and pleading the blood of Christ.

In the Second World War, as the Germans were coming yet again to bomb the East End of London, an old cockney called his wife to come down quickly into the cellar to shelter there. She said she was coming. He called out again. She said, 'I can't find my teeth.' He replied, 'Don't worry about your false teeth. They're not dropping sandwiches, they're dropping real bombs!'

The devil is dropping real dynamite, really destroying multitudes by drink, homosexuality, dirty books, drugs, violence, adultery, greed, worldliness and materialism. But we are more than conquerors through Jesus. God 'forgave us all our sins, having cancelled the written code with its regulations, that was against us, and that stood opposed to us; he took it away, nailing it to the cross, and disarming powers and authorities, triumphing over them by the cross' (Colossians 2:13-15).

After an old Scottish doctor had passed away, his wife discovered certain accounts in his book marked 'Forgiven – too poor too pay'. She tried to collect these accounts by going to court, but the judge ruled that she could never demand the debts her husband had forgiven.

Likewise, men are too poor to pay for their sins, but the Great Physician, upon our confession of our poverty and need, writes, 'Forgiven – too poor to pay'. And when Christ states that, there can be no accusing finger or demand upon us.

I gave him a crown of thorns – he gave me a crown of righteousness.

I gave him a cross to carry – he gave me a yoke which is easy.

I gave him nails through his hands – he gave me safely into his Father's hands, from which no power can pluck me.

I gave him a mock title – he gave me a new name written down in glory.

I gave him no covering, but stripped him of his clothes – he gave me the garment of salvation.

I gave him vinegar to drink – he gave me the living water.

I crucified him and slew him – he gives me life eternal and abundant.

It was my sinfulness that put him there on the cross.
It was his sinlessness that put us into grace today!

Thank God for Golgotha. Thank God for the blood of Jesus. Thank God he went into Hades, gave gifts unto men, set captives free, spoiled principalities and powers, rose again on the third day.

This revival is seeing a return to the blood of Christ. The more I preach the blood and the cross, the more sinners are converted, and the more sick people are mightily healed. The truths of the Reformation have been forgiven. The great evangelical doctrines, the jewels of Scripture, have been minimized or by-passed. We need a return to Pentecost. The church needs to be born again. The body of Christ needs to rediscover and proclaim with new passion the glorious power of the blood of Christ. Let the blood mark you!

The committed, repentant, born-from-above believer is blood-marked forever. The blood does a deep, deep work. The nightmares of hell and death are gone forever. You are made clean in mind, soul, spirit and body! Every evil imagination is forever thrown down.

MARKED BY JESUS

Let Jesus mark you forever! I am seeing thousands accepting Christ, leaving their whisky-drinking, their night-clubbing, their bingo-hall binges, their porn shop visits, cancelling their divorce court suits, burning the tablets, drugs and glue-sniffing cans, throwing away their witchcraft trinkets, *and bending low at Calvary*, and rediscovering that the blood of Christ has not lost its ancient touch. For if you accept Christ the flames of hell can never, never touch you, for you can never, ever perish.

Repentance is a conscious decision, a turning away from the old life. Then we come under the power of the blood, and every stain, every dark blot of guilt, every shame and every unclean habit is wiped away. You will never be disappointed by Jesus Christ, as you begin the adventure of faith. Christ's death turns away the anger of God. As we kneel at the foot of the cross, human nature is transformed. I've seen prostitutes, robbers, wild Bikers and hardened criminals changed. I've seen mayors, politicians, doctors, actors, sports personalities and businessmen born again. I've seen Muslims, Hindus, Sikhs, Rastafarians and Buddhists own Jesus Christ as Lord of their lives.

'He was led as a lamb to the slaughter.' Here is the heart of true, original, apostolic, biblical Christianity. His death is the key to the kingdom, the door by which we enter. His death is the death which you and I deserved to die. Calvary is the highway home. The offering of Calvary is enough to cover all human sin.

I urge our crowded congregations to fix their gaze on Calvary, to touch the hem of Jesus' garment. He is the power, he is the unique, special, only Saviour for our sins, he is the Healer Divine!

Jesus, through his blood, breaks a million chains and sets you free. The healing virtue of Jesus can flow into you. Multitudes are flocking to him in some parts of Britain and Europe.

Untold miracles are happening. Diseases of all descriptions are melting away. Thousands of poor, neglected souls are being saved, as we proclaim the message of the cross. What unspeakable pleasure and joy to announce the glorious Good News of the precious blood of Calvary.

8

FEATURES OF REVIVAL

In this chapter I want to discuss some of the main features of the revival which is presently happening across Britain.

AN AWARENESS OF GOD

First, there is an intensified awareness of God. He seems so close. We expect to see angels in our meetings. Healings and miracles have become almost commonplace.

An absorbing, overwhelming divine presence is gripping us. For the Christian who is living in the shadow of God's presence, this life is no longer a cul-de-sac but a road of hope, because God has taken up residence here. Gerard Manley Hopkins' great poem 'God's Grandeur' puts it so well:

The world is charged with the grandeur of God.
It will flame out, like shining from shook foil . . .
And for all this, nature is never spent;
There lives the dearest freshness deep down things.

The Spirit falls, and suddenly an entire congregation, or even a whole district are awakened to find that they are caught up in a movement of great spiritual destiny.

In Harborne in Birmingham even Hindus greeted me in the street due to the local revival there. One afternoon I saw an Indian closing his shop – it was only 4.30 p.m.! That was a miracle of revival! He told me, 'Very Reverend Banks, I close my shop now, I come to meeting tonight. My wife got better after your meeting last night. We are all very happy now, since Jesus come into our hearts. We want to get early seat, make sure we get in. See you later!'

In Winson Green I was welcomed like an old friend into Sikh homes, and there I saw the young people reading the Bible with great awe and excitement.

In this revival people get filled with God, and begin to live a changed life. There is great fear of God, wonder and assurance. People feel the presence of the King of Love.

After being in many meetings recently, one impression has left itself upon me: I knew I was in the presence of the King of Kings! When revival comes, people sense the awesome presence of God in a way they have never done before.

Someone has commented about recent revival meetings: 'I have never been in the presence of royalty, but the feeling I got was of standing in the presence of an unseen Ruler. I didn't know whether to stand, kneel or weep, to speak or be silent.'

The need of the church is undoubtedly to open themselves to the flow of the Holy Spirit, without whom the church is a mere shell. Apart from the Holy Spirit there can be no Christianity and no church. Worship is idolatry unless the Spirit flows through it. No local church can live up to Christ's expectations unless it gives room for the Spirit to work in its midst.

Secondly, there is a rehabilitation of evangelical truth. There is a return to an appreciation of the power of the cross.

This is an outpouring of the Spirit that leads to holiness and purity. Isaiah 35:8-9 says: 'And a highway will be there; it will be called the Way of Holiness. The unclean will not journey on it; it will be for those who walk in that Way; wicked fools will not go about on it. No lion will be there, nor will any ferocious beast get up on it; they will not be found there.'

The Lord is hard at work putting purity and holiness into us. There is a rediscovery of the old truths of God. The liberals, the radicals, the modernists, the carnal and the unspiritual are losing ground, influence and power.

Bible preaching is bringing biblical results. God is helping us to reshape what we say. We are relearning that 'he upholds all things by the Word of his power.' The truths long forgotten or only echoed by a few in the land need to be re-echoed like a trumpet call: truths such as the second coming, repentance, restitution, the discipled life, obedience to the Word, faith, belief in the accuracy of the Bible, and holiness and purity of life. Many are getting hold of these scriptural truths and are taking off like a rocket. You get top priority if you get some Word in you! There is a new joy, earnestness and seriousness about the things of the Word.

CHANGED LIVES

Thirdly, there is an enhanced standard of conduct. The most impressive effect of revival is changed lives. Selfish living is giving way to love. The church's mission is not only preaching and healing, but also feeding the poor, housing the homeless, delivering the demon-possessed, succouring the old, and caring for the widows.

SENSITIVITY TO SIN

Fourthly, there is an acute sensitivity to sin. Great conviction of unchecked wickedness is the order of the day. I often see weeping in my meetings. The Word of God is falling like lead on the hearers.

There is also an emphasis that in Christ all sin is gone, that there are no half-salvations. As Corrie Ten Boom said, 'He has taken all my sins away, and cast them into the depths of the sea, and on the shoreline he has posted a sign saying, "No fishing".'

God has removed the sins of all those who trust in his Son. He has obliterated them, he has wiped them out and they are clean gone.

Jesus saves his people from their sins. Face up to it – sin is slavery; it destroys, torments and pollutes. Yet Christ is all-powerful. Listen to his voice, look to his passion. Fall at his feet, make his cross your hiding-place. There we find cleansing, purging, forgiveness and healing.

G. K. Chesterton wrote, 'Sin is the most demonstrable of all Christian doctrines.' Solomon said in Ecclesiastes, 'In this world you will find wickedness where justice and right ought to be.' But sin came through the fall of our first parents, and that special relationship that they had with God was lost. So man is under the effect of that curse up to this very hour. As Paul cried, 'Who will deliver us from this body of death?' Man has become cut off from God by his sinfulness. 'Men loved darkness rather than light.' We see in our land the cancerous spread of unfaithfulness, the break-up of family life, lusting for new mates, heart-break and sorrow. Evil waxes worse and worse. People are drugged by the world's addictions – TV, money-making, materialism, worldliness, permissiveness and pleasure-loving. We must show our nation its sin!

PRAYER A PRIORITY

Fifthly, we see an absorbing concentration on prayer. It is difficult for me to get my son Philip to eat – he is so busy praying! As I write this, he is on another seven-day fast. No wonder heaven is coming down! God is honoured when people depend on him for everything.

When I was working in the south of France, I stopped in the little village on the outskirts of Cannes where Picasso lived most of the latter years of his life. I was on a crusade tour in the area, and was most inter-ested in this strange character who outraged society with his pictures. There I stared at his painting of a table. The legs didn't join up, the sides were like the front, the corners were inside out and the table-top was upside down. As you focus on it, all topsy-turvy, you see, however, what he wanted to portray. As you study it for some time, instead of a mish-mash, it begins to take shape; you surprisingly see the impossible. For here before your eyes you see a table from every point – something you could not do if looking at one in reality.

In prayer we are taken into an extraordinary dimen-sion. Here the divine Artist opens our eyes. When we pray our Lord and Saviour Jesus Christ reveals to us things we could never see otherwise; we see the world from his perspective. Then we are able to begin to do the same works and extraordinary accomplishments that he did.

It is indeed like looking at a Picasso. How many, after the Scriptures are proclaimed, say, 'Why, I never saw it that way before!' We move into a supernatural, divine dimension. It's not revealed to us by flesh and blood but by our Father in heaven.

'Not by might, nor by power, but by my Spirit, saith the Lord.' God wants to reveal himself to ordinary people today. He wants Christians to walk in his might and power. He wants to open our eyes to his unceasing wonders. He wants us to share his works and rout his enemies. The same dying Saviour who was resurrected from the dead reaches down through the centuries to us today. His wisdom, revelation, light, gifts, abilities and powers are offered to us. We can win, we can conquer, we can achieve the impossible in our lives, our homes, our families and our society. All of this can happen through red-hot, Holy Ghost, constant, crying, beseeching, loving intercession.

A NEW LOVE FOR THE CHURCH

Sixth, there is a new love for the church. Some are now giving all for it. No more Sunday Christianity for them! I know some who have even sold their homes to give money to the poor, to evangelize the world, to open new churches, to spread the gospel, to house the homeless. School teachers, doctors, businessmen, university lecturers and dentists are giving up lucrative jobs to go out and live freely as servants of the people, to bring the Good News of Jesus to lost towns, dark areas and poverty-struck lands. There is a new abandonment in worship. We are giving the church back to Christ. He is in charge. He is having pre-eminence amongst us.

Seventhly, there is an exciting realization of unity. There is a new love for all God's people. The denominational barriers are coming down. Where they are raised again, the blessing has gone!

There has been much emphasis on empire-building, on 'my' church or 'our' denomination. Where unity has been mentioned, it has excited more division than there was before! Ecumenical wheeling and dealing has failed. Empty outward signs of unification have come to nothing.

God hates formalities. He loathes ecclesiastical shows and religious ceremonies. Two little boys were once talking on the front row just prior to a service. They said, 'We go to different churches, we belong to different abominations'!

Religious pretence wearies God. 'Your new moons and appointed feasts my soul hateth . . . I am weary to bear them' (Isaiah 1:14). God hates clap-trap, boring monologues, half-hearted prayers, meaningless rituals and traditions. 'Ye have wearied God with your words' (Malachi 2:17). 'By your words shall you be justified and by your words shall you be judged . . . every idle word, they shall give account of in the day of judgement' (Matthew 16:36-37).

Thank God that name-calling is receding, that there is a new longing to join forces with all of God's people, to break through in our society, to fulfil our Lord's command to show our united love for lost man and to win them all for Christ.

Eighthly, there is a new, augmented inspiration in evangelism. Real, heart-felt passion is slowly reappearing. It caused John Wesley to jump on his horse and ride out to save the world. It caused Jackie Pullinger to walk into the dreaded Walled City of Hong Kong and pull down Satan's strongholds. It caused Reinhardt Bonnke to rush out to Africa and sweep millions of souls into the Kingdom of God.

It causes many unknown people, young and old, from all walks of life, to rise up to take Christ to the unsaved people of our day. What we see now is a bold church.

SOCIAL JUSTICE

Ninthly, we see a passion for social justice. I see a new humanitarian concern for the poor, the aged, the sick, the suffering, the broken and the underprivileged of our world. One church which I helped to plant has recently taken yet another articulated lorry full of medical supplies, food, clothes and many other aids to Romania. This must be their tenth trip with such a consignment! Many other churches are doing similar work.

Love is a choice. It creates a high-trust climate. Such an atmosphere is one that anticipates growth both spiritually and numerically in our local churches. That love can be expressed in prayer, of course, for it is an expression of our love for humanity and our devotion to Christ. Yet without some practical expression of that love, we are often leaving God to do work which he has left to us.

'Go into all the world,' he said, not, 'Ask My Father

to send the Spirit to all the world.' That has already been done! Whatever our world is, we should boldly go to pray, serve, love and communicate with our words and deeds.

There are so many practical ways for us to express God's love. People involved in the revival are helping the homeless, supporting drug addicts and alcoholics as they get free from their addictions, caring for the elderly, helping one-parent families, supporting those who have had nervous breakdowns and reaching out with the gospel to the ethnic minorities.

9

REVIVAL AND PRAYER

Next door to the large Assembly of God church in Coventry is the popular pub, 'The Admiral Lord Rodney'. It sells real ale, and people come from miles around. The publican is well mannered, cheerful, smart and very well liked. He has had to extend his pub due to the great increase in patrons. He got on well with the two likeable pastors at the church.

Then when revival broke out recently, something remarkable happened. The pub patrons, who normally took little notice of the church next door, suddenly became interested in it as hundreds of people flocked to it. Most of them were from non-church backgrounds, and many of them were Hindus, Sikhs and Muslims attending their first meeting ever in a Christian place of worship. Each night of the mission the pub-goers saw the huge crowds and the long lines of taxis queueing up outside. They saw many people being lifted up the steps of the church building, and then at the end of the meetings so many of them came waltzing down the steps with rapturous joy on their faces!

Soon, at about the same time each night, quite a crowd gathered outside the pub to witness the amazing goings-on at the church. Holding their drinks in their hands, they watched mesmerized as night after night people emerged from the church carrying their sticks and crutches and walking freely.

Soon many of the pub patrons went to the meetings

themselves to see what it was all about, and some of them were converted. The whole district was talking about the signs, wonders and miracles.

The world looks up and takes notice when God's church moves with power. One night the manager of the city's football team sent his million-pound player down to have prayer for his cartilage. He got healed and converted!

The world often knows where revival is more than many Christians do! The world soon recognizes a praying, powerful church. These mighty signs were made possible through the earnest prayer of the local Christians. Prayer is a vital part of our relationship with the personal God.

Jesus said: 'If you remain in Me and My words remain in you, ask whatever you wish, and it will be given you' (John 15:7).

PRAYING AGAINST EVIL

The devil is a coward, yet we should not underestimate his power. A little girl was once asked if she was frightened when the devil knocked at her heart's door. She replied, 'No, I just send Jesus to answer the door!' This is what prayer does – it challenges the strength of evil.

Not long ago I led a mission in Hastings, the witchcraft centre of the UK. Adverts in the shop windows said, 'Learn how to be a witch'. There are many occult shops there doing a booming business. Yet hundreds packed the school hall where the mission was held. The devil was sent scurrying! Miracles happened that showed witchcraft to be ludicrous, silly nonsense with no power. Jesus' words came true through prayer: 'I give you power over all the power of the enemy.' The whole of Hastings talked about the power of Jesus Christ today. It was amazing!

Prayer today can defeat the works of the occult, just as Elijah's prayer on Mount Carmel showed the priests of Baal to be utterly powerless.

Consider the prayers of the Bible: Elijah shut up the heavens so that they gave no rain (1 Kings 17:1); Jesus, in prayer in the garden of Gethsemane, won the battle of Golgotha (Luke 22:41-46); the prophet Agabus prepared the Jerusalem Christians for the time of famine (Acts 11:28-30); Peter was delivered from prison as the church prayed (Acts 12); and Paul and his companions were saved out of a shipwreck (Acts 27:21-25).

By prayer in the name of Jesus, Christians can bring a spirit of deep conviction of sin upon our nation, a great revulsion against the wickedness which has for so long defiled and degraded it. The people will cry out, as others did on the day of Pentecost, 'Brothers, what shall we do?' (Acts 2:37).

We have the assurance of victory over all the powers of the evil one. The Bible tells us so – in fact, the supremely important message of this remarkable book is that 'heaven rules' and 'the Most High is sovereign over the kingdoms of men' (Daniel 4:17,25-26,34). This is a marvellous and encouraging word for Christians today, but what a sobering message for the world!

So when we pray, we are immediately involved in the affairs of the heavenly realm. By the ministry of the Holy Spirit through the Word and prayer, we can learn something of God's purposes and intentions, and we can co-operate with him in them.

We strive in prayer against the hosts of wickedness in

heavenly places; we fight against the principalities and powers, and we battle at the very gates of hell. As we fight under the banner of the Crucified One, we have the assurance of victory over all the powers of the evil one.

PRAYING DAY AND NIGHT

Individual believers like Daniel, or a group of believers gathered together in the name of Jesus, can powerfully affect other individuals, churches and even nations for God.

We remember that Joshua restrained the sun from going down (Joshua 10:12-13). That is a type of praying that the church in Europe knows nothing about!

The shadow of Peter healed the sick. Something has to happen to God's people today if we are to see this type of holy power. How weak, watery, heartless, strengthless and powerless the British church is today! The Christians who are involved in the present revival are praying night and day: consequently they are seeing amazing miracles. As Scripture says: 'And may these words of mine, which I have prayed before the Lord, be near to the Lord our God day and night' (1 Kings 8:59).

Somehow, it seems, God has a way of holding our prayers before his gaze 'day and night'. It is also possible for us to be in prayer day and night. Ask God to equip you, by his Spirit, to be in prayer at all kinds of times, consciously or otherwise. Let prayer become your life-style!

In California a few years ago there was a chain of restaurants built to look like windmills. They were eye-catching and attractive, and the food was good too. At first, I thought the Americans had bought up the old windmills of Holland or East Anglia, but when I got close I could see that they were made of fibreglass! The wind could blow to hurricane force, and those sails would still not turn. Many British churches and Christians are like that. They look all right at first glance, but on closer inspection you discover that they are only made of plastic. Though the Spirit is blowing freely and strongly as we approach the end, they still refuse to be filled by him and to function in prayer. Let's circle the nation with victory praying!

The apostle Paul observed that God 'is able to do immeasurably more than all we ask or imagine' (Ephesians 3:20). What God can do is infinitely beyond our highest prayers, desires, thoughts or hopes.

A man once said that his philosophy of life was, 'Don't hurry, don't worry, and stop and smell the flowers.' To which I can only add, 'and take it to the Lord in prayer'. Prayer can and should become your way of life. If there is no way, God will make a way. Do not delay: start today. Pray without ceasing!

THE IMPORTANCE OF PRAYER

That much–loved and prolific writer on prayer, Edward McKendree Bounds, declares, 'The most important lesson we can learn, is how to pray.' Gordon Cove called prayer 'the greatest unused force in the world'. S. D. Gordon says, 'The great people of the earth today are the people who pray.'

Larry Lea, who built up a church from 13 people to 7,000 through prayer, was taught by the Spirit to pray the Lord's Prayer really slowly. Thus began a phrase-by-phrase praying that was amplified as he went along by the Holy Spirit showing him things to pray about and people to pray for. Some of my friends have found the Holy Spirit leading them in exactly the same way to prayer. This resulted in some staggering answers to prayer.

Thomas Payne describes prayer as 'a force which is infinitely greater than the world has ever yet dreamed'. Reuben A. Torrey makes no bones about it; he says there is a 'need for constant, persistent, sleepless, over-coming prayer . . . *because there is a devil*' (his emphasis, not mine). An unknown Christian writes, 'We are never so high as when on our knees.' L. A. T. van Dooren says, 'You will learn to pray as you pray, and as you pray, so you will come to know the meaning of true prayer.' Warren Wiersbe writes, 'If a person is truly born again prayer will be as natural as breathing.' Abraham Lincoln prayed 'that I may receive that Divine assistance, without which I cannot succeed, but with which success is certain'. Mr Lincoln spent every morning from 4 o'clock to 5 o'clock in reading the Scriptures and praying.

DEPENDING ON GOD

God is teaching us that we should no longer try to accomplish things in the flesh by natural power and ability, but by dependence on him. We are seeing a revival of faith, a revival of love, a revival of holiness. This intercession gives us a greater God-consciousness and victory in the intensified conflict between light and darkness, good and evil, faith and doubt. God is calling us to faithful prayer, fervent prayer, effective prayer. Draw near to God; seek him for his glory alone.

We must learn from the successful, victorious

113

winners and warriors of the past. 'Elijah stepped forward and prayed . . . "O Lord, answer me, so these people will know that You, O Lord, are God and that You are turning their hearts back again." Then the fire of the Lord fell' (1 Kings 18:36-38).

Before uttering this prayer Elijah confronted false religion and idolatry by taking on the prophets of Baal and Asherah. He was against evil, but for the people. We, too, should take our stand against the devil's schemes before praying urgently for God's revelation of himself to others.

'Then he stretched himself out on the boy three times and cried to the Lord, "O Lord my God, let this boy's life return to him!" The Lord heard Elijah's cry and the boy's life returned to him' (1 Kings 17:21-22). We sometimes forget that miracles did not start and finish with the ministry of Jesus. If you are praying for something you think is impossible, look to God, and remember that with him all things are possible!

Recently a woman who had been totally blind had her sight restored – and it was recorded by TV cameras! In the same programme another woman walked from her wheelchair. The ITV interviewers were dumbfounded! This TV programme started a media debate throughout the South of England. Through it the miraculous power of God was brought to the attention of the public. Prayer works miracles that eventually reach millions!

The world has been waiting to see the sons of God come into their own. We are the representatives of Christ. The world is waiting to see the power of God today. People need uplifting. People need to feel and see God's power!

God has broken in on us. Revival is the return of the

anointing. Go for great things; rivers of Divine truth are flowing. A half-open heart will only get half of the blessing. Be open to heaven. God is ready, willing, working and giving. A breakthrough in the supernatural has begun – by prayer!

WHAT JESUS SAID ABOUT PRAYER

Students of the New Testament cannot fail to notice that Christ speaks about prayer in two ways. Sometimes he seems clearly to imply that anything can be had for the bare asking, that there is no need to cry and plead and agonize, that all that is necessary is, as it were, to stretch out the hand and take what God wishes to give. At other times, however, Jesus teaches with equal clarity that true prayer often involves a tremendous struggle, that it calls for insistence and persistence and demands a desperate earnestness if it is to gain what it desires.

That is what the saints have found. 'We prevail with men by importunity,' observes Matthew Henry, 'because they are displeased with it, but with God because he is pleased with it.' Murray McCheyne, the young Scottish saint, had this in mind when he confessed, 'It takes me half an hour to get an audience with God: half an hour to fight my way through.'

The desperateness of prayer! Jesus pointed to that when he told the story of the poor widow who pestered the unjust judge until he granted her redress. He touched on the same topic when he spoke of the man shamelessly hammering on his friend's door at midnight, clamouring for three loaves so violently that at last the reluctant householder got up and gave them to him. He talked of the same thing when he remarked to the distracted disciples, baffled in their attempts to liberate the demoniac lad, 'This kind cometh not out but by prayer.'

Nor was it only by what he said that Christ called attention to this aspect of prayer. He illustrated it still more strikingly in action. J. B. Phillips, in his admirable translation of the Epistles of the New Testament, has a graphic rendering of Hebrews 5:7: 'Christ, in the days when He was a man, appealed to the One who could save Him from death in desperate prayer and the agony of tears.' We shall never know the intensity of that terrific crisis. We may never know the anguished intercession of Gethsemane. We may never know that grim grappling of the Redeemer with his Father's will, of which a modern poet has daringly said:

> For in that desperate hour
> God fought God,
> And all the lights of heaven were afraid.

Yet we may, in our way, know something of importunate prayer, the prayer of crisis, the prayer which accomplishes great things. Do you pray like that?

I like the old story of Ian McPherson:

Once, in the course of a journey from South Wales to Scotland, the train on which a friend was travelling halted for a time just outside Shrewsbury Station. Opposite him in the compartment were two little boys. One had his nose glued to the glass of the window and was staring out impatiently, obviously waiting for the train to start. The other was tinkering with the button of the bell one rings to summon the attendant. After standing for what seemed an age, the engine suddenly gave a sharp whistle and the carriages jumped to attention as the great locomotive began to move. 'Hurrah!' shouted the first little fellow, 'we're off!' 'Of course,' sniffed the other, with an air of great knowledge and self-importance, 'didn't you see me press the button?'

Some would try to persuade us that there is no more real relation between our prayers and what happens in the world than between the pressing of the bell-push and the movement of the train.

Truth often becomes clearer after five minutes' prayer than after five hours' reasoning. I stood once in Copenhagen Cathedral just under Thorwalden's magnificent marble statue of Christ. Then I suddenly remembered that to see the true beauty of the face of that figure you must get on your knees. Truth is like that. You see it best in the posture of devotion.

PRAYER IS PROFITABLE

Prayer is profitable because it makes power available. Man loves power and adopts all sorts of expedients to acquire it. He amasses money, he acquires learning, he achieves fame – all in an effort to gain power. According to the most brilliant psychologist in the modern world, power is man's basic demand, the thing which he most passionately desires. God has made man that way. He has made him to want power. And more, God himself provides the power for which his creature craves. One of the ways in which he communicates that power is prayer. In prayer we link our impotence to his omnipotence, and we are thus able to cry with the apostle, 'I can do all things through Christ who keeps pouring power into me.' That is a wonderful translation of that verse, and it speaks of a wonderful experience. As we pray, God pours power into us, and thus we have practical proof of the profit of prayer.

Prayer is profitable because it makes sin impossible. There are, in this regard, only two alternatives: either sinning will make a man stop praying or praying will make him stop sinning. Praying and sinning are mutually exclusive. They cannot co-exist in a human heart. It must be either the one or the other. The American missionary John Hyde said, 'One sin costs us the presence of God.' That remark may not be theologically profound, but it is strangely memorable nevertheless, because it is so transparently true. To try to pray effectually whilst nursing known sin is like trying to get through to someone on the telephone when the wire has been cut. It doesn't matter how loudly you shout, you won't be heard, for the living link has been severed. And when you pray regularly, systematically and devotedly you help to make it impossible for you to lapse into habitual sin.

Many Christians today seem to be unconcerned about the unsaved people around them. But we desperately need a prayer breakthrough to reach the lost millions. Such a prayer breakthrough will not be easy; it will require a greater commitment to prayer in our own lives. If you want to experience an avalanche of God's power in your life and in your community, if you want to see the devil's strongholds pulled down, then you must commit yourself to a prayer breakthrough.

People with a vision are driven by the desire to see God shake comfortable, traditional Christianity from the roots up with a revival of committed, fervent prayer.

God wants his church to be both a *praying people* and a *powerful people*. Paul wrote, 'I never cease to give thanks for you when I mention you in my prayers' (Ephesians 1:16). He was so thrilled that the Ephesians had come to faith through his ministry (Acts 19), and he continued his ministry by praying for them. No wonder Paul's pastoral ministry was so blessed. What a prayer warrior he was! He longed for his converts to grow into men and women of stature; he wanted them to possess the rich inheritance which was theirs in Christ.

Here we see the inextricable link between growth and prayer. You show me a church which believes that God answers prayer and which waits on him with a sense of urgency and commitment, and you have shown me a growing, vibrant church. You show me a Christian who is steeped in prayer, who puts aside a chunk of time each day for the study of Scripture and the soaking of that study in prayer, and you have shown me a growing and effective Christian.

Prayer and evangelism must go hand in hand. We may pray and pray for all we're worth, but unless there is the willingness to work to bring in the harvest (Luke 10:2), we may never see the results of the prayer. More often than not, the opposite has been the case. We've worked very hard at trying to win people for Christ, and seen so little lasting fruit for our labours. We may have organized, planned, run conferences, given generously, set up structures, and still not have achieved much.

The real question is whether we will learn these biblical lessons that are both being demonstrated before our eyes as well as being recorded in the history of revivals. The whole church must rediscover the necessity of being alone with God on the hilltop, and not leaving the task of prayer to the few. The whole church must set out to rob the strong man of his goods – he won't let them go until we take them! This is not the work of just a few evangelists but of the whole church.

Revival is not just a question of history. It is happening today. If we look at the parts of the world that are experiencing rapid church growth, we would be forced to admit that one thing is very clear: there is a harnessing of prayer with evangelism. Revival is clearly related to fervent and sacrificial prayer.

At 15 years of age he recorded in his diary that he had begun to pray three times each day – twice for an hour and once for 15 minutes! With that beginning, it is not surprising that at the age of 27 he, Count Zinzendorf, led the community that he had built into a movement of prayer that was to last for 100 years! And the result? The Moravian Brethren movement began. It was to send missionaries all over the world.

You may not believe that you, as a person, could pray that many times a day, or for that long. That's not the point. The point is, do you want to see a major spiritual awakening amongst the young people in this nation? Do you want to see your friends come to know Christ? Do you want to be part of a big change in your school, college or place of work? You do? Great! But you'll never do it through wishing, hoping or even witnessing alone. You will see it come about through prayer – passionate, powerful, persistent, extraordinary prayer. Prayer will bulldoze through the barriers, move the mountains and shake the powers of darkness.

The great revivalist Charles Finney used to say, 'The church can have a revival whenever it wants it, providing it is willing to pay the price.' There is a certain amount of truth in that statement. The history of revival shows that whenever God is about to send revival, he 'sets his people a-praying'. John Wesley said, 'God does nothing redemptively in the world – except through prayer.' So although revival is a sovereign act of God, it flows down from heaven to earth along the channel of fervent, believing prayer.

Although it is only by the Holy Spirit that revival can come, and it cannot be drummed up by man, we must not conclude that man has nothing to do with it. There is a part for us to play.

In revival, there is God's part, and ours. God's part is to hear true prayer; to respond to it; to see our passion; and to respond with like passion by sending the Spirit, in order to bring tremendous conviction of sin; to utterly change the life and outlook of man.

Our part is to pray to God fervently. Such prayer is very different from the trivial, shopping-list type of prayer which is so prevalent today. We must treat fervent prayer as an absolute priority.

In Isaiah 35:5-7 God promises that signs and wonders will accompany revival: 'Then will the eyes of the blind be opened and the ears of the deaf unstopped. Then will the lame leap like a deer, and the mute tongue shout for joy. The burning sand will become a pool, the thirsty ground bubbling springs. In the haunts where jackals once lay, grass and reeds and papyrus will grow.' This is happening for his glory in our land!

Either we do want revival, or we don't. A wistful

wishing for it is an insult to God. A rugged pressing on for it is a pleasure to him. We have to choose, *now*.

When an arm came off Rita's doll, she toddled indoors from the garden. 'Mummy mend it,' said she. Again, 'Will you mend it, Mummy?' The little one had complete confidence in her mother; she was sure that Mummy not only could but also would mend it.

When Jesus said, 'of such is the Kingdom of God' he meant, I think, that you and I are to be like children, telling God our need, and knowing he will help us.

Most of us at some time have come to the end of our resources, and then have discovered that at the right time and in the right way God met our need. He was neither slow nor tardy. So don't be discouraged, Christian. Keep on claiming the promises. God is the faithful promiser. Our future is as bright as God's promises.

Here is my advice to Christians today: Turn off the TV, cancel the papers, disconnect the telephone, and seek God till he falls upon you!

The Gospels are full of the promises of Jesus. No other leader has ever made such amazing promises, and he has kept every one.

God's got a best plan for each life. It's wonderful to be his totally, it's wonderful to be part of his Kingdom. Jesus' life was matchless, his word is unbreakable, he is true to his covenant, his character is immensely attractive, his is the greatest teaching ever given to mankind. So often Jesus stops me in my tracks and astounds me! What extravagant love! The very brightness of Jesus' life shows up the dark corners of our own. He cleanses, purifies and empowers whoever comes into contact with him.

10

REVIVAL AND FAITH

The secret of spiritual greatness is faith. Have you ever considered what faith really is? Here's one acrostic definition of faith: 'Forsaking All, I Trust Him'. Scripture says, 'Now faith is being sure of what we hope for and certain of what we do not see' (Hebrews 11:1, NIV).

Winston Churchill said, 'I am bewildered by the world, the confusion is terrible, I attribute it in part . . . to that great decay in belief . . . it's bad for a nation when it is without faith.' What is true of society in general is also true of the church. Our problem is a deep lack of faith.

God will do anything for the man or woman of faith. God will move heaven and earth for faith. God will cause the rivers to run backwards for faith. God will cause the sun to stand still for faith. God will move mountains for faith. God will make iron swim for faith. God will do the impossible for his children of faith!

Elisha asked Elijah for twice as much power as that which was shown by his master. Did he receive it? It is recorded that Elisha performed exactly twice as many miracles as did Elijah. He seemed to have more power in his dead bones than many of us have in our living bones!

What is the great secret to God's miracles of faith and power? The answer lies succinctly in the dynamic and creative teaching of Jesus Christ: 'Everything is possible for him who believes' (Mark 9:23). As you learn faith and train your heart and mind to believe, defeatist tendencies are reversed and everything moves out of the area of the impossible into that of the possible.

Many Christians today have mislaid the key that opens the door to the Kingdom – faith. Faith is a great force just waiting to be used. Faith realizes that to our Heavenly Father all is possible: 'He is able to do immeasurably more than all we ask or imagine' (Ephesians 3:20).

Faith does not doubt or hesitate. Trust in the naked Word of God. Submit to God, take his hand. Go out with faith into the unknown with full reliance on him. Give yourself away. Die within, that faith may live in you.

Do not dwell daily with doubters. Do not linger in the enemy's city, as Lot did. Do not warm your hands by the enemy's fire, as Peter did. Do not sleep in the enemy's lap, as Samson did. Surround yourself with men of faith!

MEN OF FAITH

Gideon dared everything as he cut his army down to 300 in the face of a great enemy. He dared to believe and risk everything on God's promises.

Abraham dared everything as he took his son up to slay him and offer him as a sacrifice. But God was true to his own character and blessed him.

Elijah dared everything as he boasted before the pagan priests of Baal that his God was true and would light the soaking wooden altar. God answered with fire!

A little saying I often use in my meetings goes, 'Faith never stands around with its hands in its pockets.' For faith sees the invisible, believes for the incredible and receives the impossible.

The motto outside a church in Missouri, USA, runs, 'We believe that the power behind us is greater than the task before us.' Nurture this kind of faith.

Defeat negativism. Rampant negativism is one of our greatest enemies: 'It can't be done . . . It won't work . . . I'm happy as I am . . . I'm too busy to think about these things.' Every time we speak in such a way, we are denying the new birth which Christ has given us. For Jesus was always positive. The most powerful men and women of faith are those who have overcome negative attitudes.

Two shoe salesmen were sent up the Amazon to cover different parts of the same area. After three days the first man sent a cable: 'Returning home next plane. Impossible to sell shoes here. Everybody goes barefoot.'

Nothing was heard from the second salesman for almost a month. When his cable arrived it read: 'Sales booming and prospects unlimited. Nobody has shoes here!' With every question, it all depends on how you look at it! Faith makes us bold and strong.

A Mexican prayer goes:

I am only a spark – make me a fire.
I am only a spring – make me a lyre.
I am only a drop – make me a fountain.
I am only an anthill – make me a mountain.
I am only a feather – make me a wing.
I am only a rag – make me a king.

The biggest task any believer has is to become a giant in faith. An American geologist gave up a lucrative career to become a missionary in South America. After a few years the giant corporation he had formerly worked for offered him a top position. When he refused the offer the corporation's representative gasped and could not understand how the missionary could turn down the job and with it the chance of being a wealthy man. The executive asked, 'Is the salary offer not big enough?' The missionary smiled and replied, 'No, it's not that – the job is not big enough! I have the biggest job and the greatest calling on earth to do!' And that call is to be 'great in faith'!

Prayer and faith work together. Prayer directs faith, I find. I build my faith by reading the Word night and day. Prayer is the voice of the soul, while faith is its hand. Prayer communicates with God, but only through faith are spiritual and practical victories won. Prayer knocks at the door of grace, and faith opens it. Prayer contacts God, and faith obtains an audience with him. Prayer makes a petition, and faith presses through to touch the hem of God's garment. Prayer quotes the promise, and faith proclaims the fulfilment of the promise.

MOSES – A MAN OF FAITH

Moses was a colossus in history, one of the greatest leaders of all time. He was, said Steven in Acts 7, a man 'powerful in speech and action' and 'educated in all the wisdom of the Egyptians'. He was taught the protocol of kings. He was well versed in Egypt's history and culture. The pyramids were as visible to Moses 3,500 years ago as they are to us today. Moses was brought up as the son of Pharaoh's daughter. His adoptive grandfather was treated as a god. Pharaoh was the chief unifying factor in Egyptian religious life and the chief priest of every temple. The Egyptians believed that he was the one who made the sun to rise and set, the Nile to flood and ebb, the grain to grow.

But for all his princely power and prestige, Moses refused to be called the son of Pharaoh's daughter. He chose rather to suffer affliction with the people of God than to enjoy the passing, temporary pleasures of sin (Hebrews 11:24-25).

He was to know God, love God, obey God, talk with God, and actually catch a brief glimpse of God during his lifetime. He was to get so close to God that his very face shone. He was to deliver God's Ten Commandments to the world.

If you met Moses, you would probably wonder how such a man ever became so brave and led people so well. The plain fact is that the secret of his greatness was his faith.

Hebrews chapter 11 stresses that Moses accomplished what he did 'by faith'. We are told: 'By faith, when he had grown up, he refused to be known as the son of Pharaoh's daughter . . . By faith he left Egypt, not fearing the king's anger . . . By faith he kept the Passover . . . By faith the people passed through the Red Sea as on dry land.'

We can have the same faith. Jesus said: 'If you have faith as small as a mustard seed, you can say to this mountain, "Move from here to there", and it will move. Nothing will be impossible for you' (Matthew 17:20).

Apart from inspiring us to have faith, the story of Moses surely shows us that God is often the God of second chances. Moses failed in his first attempt to serve God, and spent interminable years as a shepherd in Midian.

God will do the same for us. When we fail and stumble and are ready to quit, he will often give us a second chance. He will, I pray, inspire you to greater faith and pull you out of the Slough of Despond and on to the Celestial City.

LIVE IN THE WORD

Live in the Word day and night. This will build up your faith. Read it in your spare moments during the day, in bed before you retire, at work when having your lunch, when travelling by train or bus. I have read the Bible while on planes and boats, and even on a bike! I have read it in an oxen cart, on horseback, and while trekking through the Malaysian jungle (but keeping a sharp lookout for snakes!). Read, read, read! Switch the TV off – there's not much commonsense on it in any case. As we spend time in God's Word our faith grows, and we feel his marvellous presence in our lives.

As we operate our faith we get answers – we see changes in people, circumstances, businesses, families and churches. We also feel God's presence within us more strongly.

G. Campbell Morgan said, 'Seeing is not believing; seeing is seeing; believing is being confident, without seeing.' Augustus Toplady said, 'It is the peculiar business of faith's eye to see in the dark.' Sangster said, 'Faith places a candle in the darkest night.' C. T. Studd claimed, 'Faith in Jesus laughs at impossibilities.' William Clarke wrote, 'Faith is the daring of the soul to go farther than it can see.'

Through faith, in spite of dire darkness, God is giving to believing people a great apostolic wave of revelation and power. We are living in a time like no other. God is working miracles, God is showing us that he is still on the throne.

It is time to rise up and shake off every darkness and chain of ignorance; Jesus and his victories must become living realities. By faith all things – every evil power, every bad habit, every guilt, worry, fear, weakness, depression, sickness and sin – are conquered. This is good news!

Away with weak, lethargic, worldly, carnal, apathetic Christianity! God's message is a gospel of power! Victory is ours on the cross, Satan is defeated. Through Jesus Christ's complete work of Calvary, the curse of darkness has been dealt with and sin, anguish, disease and unrighteousness have been put away. Through faith in Jesus forgiveness, bodily healing, deliverance of mind, release from worldliness and a new life of holiness are all wonderously possible. The Word is clear: 'Through faith and patience you will inherit the promises.'

Faith is communion with God; it is building fellowship with the Father. The Word of God is the seed which produces supernatural results. 'The Kingdom of God is as if a man should scatter seed on the ground, and should sleep by night and rise by day, and the seed should sprout up and grow. He himself does not know how, for the earth yields crops by itself; first the blade, then the head and after that the full grain' (Mark 4:26-28).

The Word is alive! J. B. Phillips, when producing his famous translation of the Bible, said that as he got deeper into the original Greek and Hebrew texts, it was like rewiring a house with the mains left on!

11

THE RAIN OF REVIVAL

God is so willing, so giving, so mighty in revealing himself at this present hour. At times, when faced with the slowness of his people, he must be near to shouting at us, 'Get on with it!'

Signs and wonders will be relatively commonplace as the end draws near. In Mark 16:17, Jesus promised that 'signs' would accompany the preaching of those who believed. In Matthew 24, when asked, 'What will be the sign of your coming?' Jesus gave important indications as to what to expect. In John 14:12 he said, 'Anyone who has faith in me will do what I have been doing. He will do even greater things than these . . .'

The day of miraculous happenings is not over, and while God will not perform wonders to order, he has pledged himself to 'confirm his word by the signs that accompany it' (Mark 16:20).

Revival has become part of God's agenda. The Holy Spirit is amongst us with great power. Dr Yonggi Cho calls him 'the unrelenting pressure of God upon us'.

Peter Neilson, the Organiser for Evangelism in the Church of Scotland, sums it up in this way: 'There is spiritual awakening, structural reshaping. The bones are rattling. The wind is blowing.'

Graham Noble has written this prayer: 'Heavenly Father, grant us the grace to humble ourselves and the faith to allow your Holy Spirit complete freedom in our lives. Give us the strength to serve you in His power and to encourage and release others whatever age, sex, race or class they may be. Help us to work together with all those who love, honour and serve our Lord and Saviour Jesus Christ. Let us be a visible prophetic witness to His character and power, an evidence that He is alive and well amongst His people today. Amen.'

As Paul put it: 'The weapons we fight with are not the weapons of the world. On the contrary, they have divine power to demolish strongholds' (2 Corinthians 10:4).

The weakness of man with the 'powers of heaven' are a formidable combination. When will we learn that? The secret is total submission to God. It is essential to realize that our loyalty is first to God, his Word and our own conscience. Then God is able to use us more in the ways of Scripture.

But are all sincere when seeking revival? Are not many jumping on the bandwagon, merely because of the sensational happenings? Do we really mean it when we say, 'I want to be in on the revival also'?

PRAYING FOR RAIN

Faced with the dreadful spiritual drought of our time, and the appalling dearth of real religion, we Christians sometimes pray for the rain of revival. But do we really mean it? Are we desperately concerned about the prevailing conditions, are we in earnest in our prayers for spiritual reawakening and renewal? Do we yearn above all things for a sight of the cloud like a man's hand? And do we really believe that the rain will come?

John Henry Jowett tells how once in his home in Birmingham he made a little paper water-mill for his child. Placing it beneath the tap and turning it on, he watched the toy working as the water provided the motive power. And he says it was a strange thing to him to reflect that the rain which, some time before, had fallen on the grey crests of the Welsh mountains, was now available in his home for that modest use. God's spiritual rain, too, is immediately available. It is 'laid on' for our need.

Do you recall that dramatic narrative in the Old Testament, where Elijah and his servant were scaling the slopes of Carmel? Presently the prophet cast himself down on the earth, his head between his knees, in an agony of intercession. He was praying for the ending of the drought and for the coming of rain. After a while he sent his servant to the summit to look out across the sea. But there was no sign. The sky was like a huge inverted bowl of burnished brass, filled with quivering heat, and the heavens were bare. Sadly, the servant returned with a negative report. But the prophet kept on praying. 'Go again seven times,' he said. The servant toiled again to the top of the mountain, and gazed out across the deep. And at last, out of the Mediterranean rose a tiny cloud, as small as a man's hand. It was enough. The cries of the man of God were about to be answered. The desolating drought was almost over. The rain was on the way.

Yes, but the point is that if the servant, instead of scanning the skies, had stood staring at the prophet, he would in all probability have missed the heavenly harbinger. It is true that the prophet had something to do with the coming of the rain. It is true that God had graciously given him a part to play in ending the drought. But the prophet could not himself produce the rain: all he could do was pray it down. For rain is heavenly in its source.

Do we not tend sometimes to look too much to the prophet instead of watching the heavens? And are there not, in fact, some foolish 'prophets' who fancy that, by working themselves up into an emotional frenzy, they can themselves manufacture the rain of revival? But the true rain of revival comes from the skies alone.

HAPHAZARD?

Nothing seems more haphazard than a shower. You see the clouds in the sky. You observe that they are black and heavy and laden with moisture, but you feel that it would be impossible to forecast exactly where the rain will fall. It seems to descend at random, without relation to any conditioning law. But that is an illusion. Actually, behind the fall of every drop there is the operation of predetermining forces. A meteorologist, if he knew all the facts and factors, would be able to predict to a nicety precisely where, when and in what proportions every drop would fall.

It is the same with the rain of revival. Certainly, it does seem to fall haphazardly. It appears to descend in the most unlikely places. Glancing back across Christian history, one does get the impression that revivals have occurred in the most fortuitous fashion. Why, for example, should it have happened among the wigwams of North America in the middle of the eighteenth century? Why should it have come to the little Welsh village of Loughour, an obscure industrial hamlet hardly noticeable on the map? Why should it have visited the Hebrides, those lonely islands off the west coast of Scotland? Why there, of all places? It all looks so accidental, so haphazard, so utterly without reference to controlling law.

Why has revival come now, and on Bikers, Gipsies, Irish Republican towns and tough working-class estates? Why is it bypassing so many large, well-programmed, wealthy churches, with fine preachers and big names in their pulpits? Why is it coming to small fellowships, hard places, unknown pastors and leaders? As Reinhardt Bonnke put it, 'Revival starts with nothing . . . it is the Word of God coming again with fresh impetus.'

It is all a mystery. Nothing we can do can earn or produce revival. No one can plan it! So with the rain of revival. It is free. We may organize expensive campaigns. We may spend money prodigally on the advertising of evangelistic efforts. But we can never buy revival. That is God's gift. Simon the sorcerer thought that the 'rain' could be bought. He offered money to Peter for the patent of Divine power. But the apostle indignantly declined it. 'Thy money perish with thee,' he cried, 'because thou hast thought that the gift of God may be purchased with money.' It cannot be bought. It is free in its bestowal.

CONDITIONS

Behind all divine visitations lies the fulfilment of certain essential conditions. What are those conditions? You will find them clearly stated in 2 Chronicles 7:14: 'If My people, which are called by My Name, shall humble themselves, and pray, and seek My face, and turn from their wicked ways; then will I hear from heaven, and will forgive their sin, and will heal their land.'

Someone told me in Australia that his father was a pious farmer, and that once during a terrible drought, when for three successive years there had been an altogether inadequate rainfall, his father had prayed that rain might descend on his land. Not long afterwards, looking into the blue heavens, he saw a cloud floating in his direction. When it was above his farm, it suddenly discharged its contents, and the result was that while all around was dry and barren, his paddocks were almost incredibly green.

Was that mere coincidence? The old farmer did not think so. He sincerely believed that although God would not tinker with his world or set aside his laws in response to the pleas of so ignorant and insignificant a person as himself, there was nevertheless some real connection between his prayer and the drenching of his land with rain.

So with revival. It comes, as we have seen, in consequence of man's compliance with certain divine conditions. And yet always the sovereignty of God is a factor in its emergence.

I travelled, not long since, on the Trans-Australian Railway across the great Nullabor Plain in the interior of that Commonwealth. It was at the end of the dry season. Never had I seen such utter desolation on so large a scale. There was not a blade of grass to be seen. Around the train on all sides stretched what can only be adequately described as a sea of land. Sometimes what looked like a cloud would appear in that copper sky, but it was only a cloud of red dust that left the land even worse than it found it. I stayed in the west for some two months, and during that time the rain fell copiously on those desert regions. The result was that when I travelled back along the same track I could hardly recognize the scenery. The whole aspect of things had changed. Green grass was carpeting what had previously been barren ground, and here and there I even caught sight of a shimmering lake.

What a transformation! The rain had made all the difference.

And would not the rain of revival make all the difference to the religious situation in the world today? Would it not, as Dr Sangster claimed, empty our overcrowded prisons, stamp out our social vice, fill our churches and bring in a hundred wonderful improvements in our way of life?

All that is thrillingly true. And yet the social effects of revival wait on personal appropriation of it. The wide desert is transformed as each buried seed beneath its barren surface responds to its drop of rain.

12

FIRE FROM HEAVEN

The night I was baptized with the Fire of the Holy Ghost, I staggered up the street, as if I were drunk!

I was recently preaching in a Baptist church in the Midlands. They had never had a miracle crusade before. They were stunned as four people in wheelchairs vacated their chairs and, one after another, walked with ease. God the Holy Spirit, the same Spirit who raised Jesus from the dead, set the people free, curing them one by one. Later, two of the church's leaders tried to diagnose the sermon, analysing my technique and method. I replied, 'There is no human explanation why, after a simple sermon, 100 people came forward to give themselves to Christ, as Saviour and Lord!' Only the Holy Spirit can achieve such results.

The man or woman who takes God at his Word leaves a large section of the church, and often it's leadership, behind. The man who walks with God in the Holy Ghost is years ahead of the rest. I am totally dependent on the Holy Spirit. If he moves, I have a whale of a time. God is waiting to build this relationship with you, which will change your life for ever.

Fire, by an inflexible law, will bite like acid to the very core, eat its way to the centre, and go on burning until there is nothing left to consume. The fire of Christ is like that. Once you let it get hold of your life, there is no stopping it. You cannot keep it at arm's length. You cannot limit its influence to the exterior of your experience. You cannot say to it, 'Thus far and no further.' Deeper and deeper into your personality it will penetrate, searching the motives, scouring the desires, burning the imagination clean, until it destroys everything that is morally combustible within you.

When the first fire is lit, it feels tolerably remote, comfortably distant, far enough away not to constitute too terrible a challenge to our inner depravity. But, as the time passes and the work of grace goes on, the fire draws nearer and nearer, burning up every trace of sin, purging the secret places of the soul. And when at last the long process is over, it has bitten its way to the innermost recesses of our being. Nothing will remain but ashes – the ashes of an utter self-immolation. But do not forget that God has promised to give us beauty for ashes. That is his bargain. Give him the ashes, and he will give you the beauty. Out of that hallowing holocaust, in which sin and self are cremated, will spring the loveliness of the everlasting Christ. Fire consumes inwardly. It is wise to cry in the words of Charles Wesley:

Refining fire, go through my heart,
Illuminate my soul;
Scatter Thy life through every part
And sanctify the whole.

Spiritual fire also spreads. In Augustine's beautiful phrase, 'One loving heart sets another on fire.' John Wesley had the same thing in mind when he formulated his famous recipe for revival: 'Get on fire for God, and the world will turn out to see you burning.'

In America they tell the story of a tiny wooden chapel in Wisconsin. The normal attendance at that chapel was very small, a bare handful sparsely sown about the pews. But one Sunday, so they say, in the depths of winter, when the snow lay thick upon the ground, something went wrong with the heating apparratus in that little chapel, and the boards about the stove caught fire. Before long the timbers were crackling and charring, and smoke and flames were billowing towards the sky. Then a strange thing happened. People started coming from near and far to see the church that was on fire! The conflagration brought a congregation.

It is a parable. Fire spreads, leaping from heart to heart, from home to home, from church to church, until the whole country is aglow with spiritual flame. That has occurred before: it can occur again. 'God of Elijah, send the fire!'

But, clearly, this is going to cost something. Fires are expensive. There is always a price to be paid. You cannot catch fire without fire catching you. That is, if it is real fire. 'Painted fire,' said Campbell Morgan, 'burns nobody.' But real fire does burn! Before going to the mission field, Henry Martyn wrote in his diary, 'Hitherto I have lived to little purpose: now let me burn out for God.' There are plenty of people who are ready to flare up, but few who are prepared to burn out. But it is only those who are ready to burn out who will set the world on fire. Are we willing to be utterly consumed? God grant that we may be!

I like this prayer of a 90-year-old minister: 'O God Almighty, who art Thyself a consuming fire; whose Eternal Son came to baptize with fire; and Whose Holy Spirit first descended upon men in a rain of fire: we beseech Thee to purge us by Thy searching flame and to kindle in us the blaze of Thy holy love: for the sake of Thy Son, our Saviour, Jesus Christ. Amen.'

So many are bound in a ritualistic Christian life, bound in a religious tradition, set in a round of evangelical activity. Sadly, many are missing God's fire! But how tragic it is, that when God wants to bring us into a new life of liberty and success, we turn our back and choose the old life again!

My friend George Jesze has been a faithful missionary to Germany for nearly 25 years, and he has also been my interpreter at hundreds of meetings in Switzerland, Austria and Germany over the past few years. In one of his articles he writes:

> We took our daughter Elizabeth to see Madame Tussaud's – the famous wax-works exhibition – in London. There we saw the original iron key of the Bastille prison in Paris, and the wax bust of Comte de Lorges who had been imprisoned there.
>
> After twenty years he was released, but being unused to freedom he begged to be allowed to go back to his cell again, where he survived for only six months.
>
> This poor man had suffered so much, he was past the desire for freedom. His cell had become his home, and he could not imagine going out into the world again. It terrified him. He chose the loneliness, sadness, despair and depression of a prison, rather than unknown freedom.
>
> Millions of people are imprisoned in their thinking and circumstances, and choose to remain in their limitations, but they learn they are losers. God wants to help us to cross the threshold to a new lifestyle. He wants us to step out of those cramped, heavy boots we've been

dragging our feet in, and step into shoes He has prepared for us. These will being a steadiness, a lightness and a direction to our steps, learning to walk in his victory. If we seek the liberty, the loosening and quickening of the fire of the Holy Ghost.

Cry to God to make you drunk with his Spirit! Don't be afraid to lose your burdens, your respectability, your criticisms, your sophistication, your settled-down attitude. Sing it, pray it, shout it – 'O Lord, send the fire on me!'

13

ORDINARY PEOPLE, EXTRAORDINARY LIVES

'God chose the foolish things of the world to put to shame the wise; God chose the weak things of the world to shame the strong. He chose the lowly things of this world and the despised things . . . and the things that are not – to nulify the things that are, so that no one may boast before him' (1 Corinthians 1:27-29).

We cannot all be apostles or prophets or evangelists, but we can all have a ministry, a task, a work to do, even a gift – and all believers are witnesses to Christ in any case. The present revival is raising up an army of ordinary people with extraordinary lives.

Having made or bought a gift for a friend or family member, we also buy a sheet of decorative paper in which to wrap our present so that it may look as attractive as possible. But we must never value a gift by the wrapping. It is the content of the parcel which really matters, and the love which prompted it.

In Shakespeare's play *The Merchant of Venice*, Antonio's friend Bassanio has to choose between three caskets in order to win his bride. One casket is of gold, another of silver, the third of lead. After much thought, he makes the right choice by selecting the leaden casket.

We are also warned in the well-known proverb that 'all that glistens is not gold'. We are not to judge by appearances, for appearances can be deceptive.

Revival often comes through surprisingly weak and frail people. God gives gold to this world – rich joy, values, power, healings and miracles – through ordinary folk who are available to be used by him.

In Acts 4:13, the apostles are described as 'unschooled', ordinary men. They had very few material possessions, but how rich they were in spiritual gifts! Remember Peter's words to the lame beggar at the Beautiful Gate of the Temple: 'Silver and gold I do not have, but what I have I give to you. In the name of Jesus Christ of Nazareth, walk!'

Remember too what Paul's critics said of him: 'His letters are weighty and forceful, but in person he is unimpressive and his speaking amounts to nothing' (2 Corinthians 10:10). But who was a greater purveyor of eternal treasure than the little tent-maker from Tarsus? He travelled hundreds of miles in wild country among even wilder men, carrying with him the unsearchable riches of Christ, and at what cost to himself!

He gladly endured, for Christ's sake and the gospel's, cold and hunger, persecution, beatings, stonings and imprisonment so that he might share that treasure with others.

They judged him by his appearance in Athens too: 'What is this babbler trying to say?' they mocked (Acts 17:18). I wonder what those scornful critics would have said if they had known that Paul's letters would be translated into virtually every known language in the world.

If the first preachers of the gospel were 'common earthenware jars', what of the early churches them-selves? Think of those great cities of the ancient world: Corinth and Ephesus were notorious hot-beds of paganism, superstition and vice. But there, in some humble Christian's home, men and women met together for worship and fellowship.

Sometimes they had to meet in secret, for few of Paul's converts were strangers to persecution. Some of them paid dearly for their faithfulness, being numbered among 'the noble army of martyrs' whom we remember in the Te Deum. Paul wrote: 'To this very hour, we go hungry and thirsty, we are in rags, we are brutally treated, we are homeless . . . Up to this moment we have become the scum of the earth, the refuse of the world' (1 Corinthians 4:11).

GOD USES FAILURES

On a wild winter evening, a minister in the north of Scotland made his way to the kirk for the evening service. He waited, but no one turned up. Everyone had decided to stay at their fireside rather than struggle through the winter wind and sleet.

The minister was tempted to return to his, but on the chance that a late-comer might arrive, he busied himself in the vestry, sorting through hymn books and setting aside those that needed repair. Then he caught up on some paperwork, and finally spent some time sitting in the empty church, saying a silent prayer for all those out on such a wild night.

Next day he learned that a fishing boat from a nearby village had been in serious trouble during the storm. The skipper feared it would be driven on to the rocks. Then, gleaming through the murk, he saw the lights of the wee kirk on the hill. That told him exactly where he was, and so he was able to steer safely into the harbour. 'Thank God there was an evening service,' he said.

And the minister too thanked God that instead of packing up and going home he had stayed on for that hour's work. What had seemed then like a waste of time may have saved the lives of four fishermen.

Success is more than numbers. God uses the seeming failures, the weak and insignificant, to save our world, time and time again. It was through ordinary men and women, through their courage and loyalty, that the Good News spread across the continents and came at last to our own land.

How much we owe to them, for they fought the good fight, they kept the faith. They were mere 'earthen vessels', but they were not empty vessels. They had been filled with the love of God, the grace of our Lord Jesus Christ, and the power of the Holy Spirit.

Christian history is full of wonderful examples of how God uses ordinary people to do extraordinary things for his kingdom. William Carey was a village cobbler who took the gospel to the people of India. Mary Slessor, a Scottish mill-girl, became a pioneer missionary in West Africa. Someone has said, 'God wants your availability more than your ability.'

The need is just as great today, for all around us are men and women who are desperately thirsty for that living water which only Jesus can give, and even a 'common earthenware jar' can carry that!

It was a joy and thrill for me to learn recently about Martin. He was sent to a police cell at Leamington Spa after a riot in Strangeways Prison. He was locked in a cell which was filthy with spit and graffiti, so he asked for water and a scrubbing brush. Then with paint and a brush he transformed its appearance. When asked why he was doing this, he told the police how Jesus had changed and cleansed his life in Strangeways.

As a result of this conversation, a policeman rang the Strangeways Chaplaincy to say that this lad had really made him begin searching for faith. He had never thought that a prisoner would make him think seriously about his own life.

What a wonderful witness! It reminds me of Paul's words: 'If anyone purifies himself of what is ignoble, then he will be a vessel for noble use, consecrated and useful to the Master of the house, ready for any good work' (2 Timothy 2:20-21).

Do not underestimate yourself in God. He sees you as bigger, greater and more invincible than you see yourself. He said to the weak, forlorn, untalented failure Gideon, 'Arise, you mighty man of valour'! 'Without me you can do nothing,' Jesus said. But he also said, 'With God all things are possible.'

EVERYONE MATTERS TO GOD

The modern European churches have largely hidden Jesus from the population. Very few churches astonish or startle people any more. But in the revival meetings people come long distances to be in Jesus' company. He was surrounded by ordinary people – soldiers, fishermen, judges, taxmen, labourers, even prostitutes. They all found his company irresistible! Jesus was a man for all types. He was marvellous company. He made God real. He never turned anyone away. Every person in the world matters to God. He wants his church to show his concern for people, to meet their needs with his love and power.

Jesus said, 'This is how everyone will be able to tell that you are my followers - by your love for one another.' Sadly, Christ's followers often do not display this love. God beckons us out of the dark night of selfishness into his love and power. We must go forth with a new, undying love. This is the foundation of the power which he wants us to experience and to manifest to the world.

There are times when I despair of the church! We see its divisions, we know its disobedience, and we experience its weakness. And we feel it within ourselves, because we are part and parcel of this divided, disobedient and weak family of God.

How God must despair of us at times, when we spurn his inheritance. But we have at our disposal the power and might and victory of Jesus! That victory is ours already, and we should be claiming it, expecting it and working for it.

Do you expect to grow as a Christian this year? What about God adding new Christians to your fellowship? Do you find your heart whispering, 'It can't be done'? Here is one missionary's advice: 'Attempt great things for God, expect great things from God.' Fervent expectation is vital if we are to feel and know God's power.

'Jesus came into Galilee preaching the Good News of God: "The time has come, the Kingdom of God has drawn near. Turn away from your sins and believe the Good News."' His first sermon included these statements: 'The spirit of the Lord is upon me to preach the Good News to the poor, to proclaim release to the captives and recovering of sight to the blind, and to set the oppressed at liberty.' It is crystal clear: the Kingdom is power. The New King James version says, 'The Kingdom is not talk but power.' Today's Christians have reversed the order and made it, 'The Kingdom is talk and not power.' That is what the man in the street thinks of the church.

Jesus came to bring healing to a broken world.

Everything is different since Jesus died: nothing is the same since he was raised from the dead! Day after day I see his resurrection power, restoring blind eyes, rejuvenating paralysed limbs, giving deaf ears sound and music again, giving new hope and health to needy people.

If we are to have Jesus' power in our lives, we must first submit to his Kingly rule. Surrender the ugly, twisted nature of your life. Give way to the marvellous person of Jesus, step by step. Realize that the human race is in dire peril – out of touch with their Maker. Believe in his limitless achievement, his earth-shaking generosity, his breathtaking boldness. He waits to hear your prayer of surrender. The powerful life is the yielded, broken, submitted life.

THE FEAR OF GOD

We need to have a healthy fear of God. We must not think of him as a benevolent provider of every little thing we desire. He is the holy God. Generous, yes, but demanding too. We must prepare the royal road for the King to come. One sign of this is the fear of God, and a true hatred of sin. 'And a highway will be there; It will be called the Way of Holiness. The unclean will not journey on it; it will be for those who walk in that Way; wicked fools will not go about on it. No lion will be there, nor will any ferocious beast get up on it; they will not be found there' (Isaiah 35:8-9). The Lord is hard at work putting holiness into us!

Revival is a searching work of God. 'When God works in revival power,' says Stephen Olford, 'he does so with great searchingness.' It is worth observing that when the Holy Spirit fell at Pentecost, tongues of fire appeared over everyone's head. That fire symbolized the searching and purifying action of God. Revival always carries with it an exposure and judgement of sin.

Many people are crying out in the revival meetings, 'I know I am in the presence of the King of Kings!' When revival comes, people sense the awesome presence of God in a way they have never experienced it before.

Christ's lordship touches every area, every relationship, and every concern of our lives. If we are willing to submit to him, any loss in life will be seen as an opportunity of giving back to God what is rightfully his and trusting him to provide what is needed.

When God told Abraham to sacrifice Isaac, he seemed to be undermining his own purposes. Isaac seemed to be the son of promise through whom God would bless the world. Yet Abraham's faith had grown strong over the years, and baffled though he must have been, he said, 'God himself will provide the lamb.'

The issue is the same for us. Can we entrust everything to God – our possessions, our job, our health, our family? Submission to God means taking our hands off what belongs to him.

If we die with Jesus, we shall also live with him, for he not only died, he rose from the dead, having broken the power of sin and death once and for all. Let's catch the excitement of those first disciples, as they met the risen Christ and encountered the explosive power of his resurrection, bringing life which would last forever.

The Spirit who raised Jesus from the dead is living in you. Give yourself away to Jesus; make him your Lord all the time. Break loose from your inner selfishness. Let the Spirit bear you along. See a breakthrough in the supernatural in your life.

God is willing, God is ready, God is working, God is unfailing. Walk in truth. Open up to heaven.

God wants us to get into action, to take the Good News to all mankind! God wants us to be a powerful people and a prayerful people. In the words of a recent prophecy: 'I desire that my people will bow the knee – not with mouth only, but from your innermost being, that My truth, My character, will be in My people. I will not withhold one of My promises from My people who will listen. I will not anoint the flesh, but the spirit. Let my Spirit come upon your spirit.'

May we all say, 'Amen, so be it!'

14

SUCCESSFUL CHRISTIAN LIVING

'What are the pathways to power?' I'm often asked this question. Many Christians want to know how they can have God working powerfully in their lives. I realize that even after nearly 40 years of preaching, I'm only just starting in the pathways of power.

The story goes of the man who got a job as a roadsweeper in the old days of brush and shovel. He asked the boss if there was any special training. The boss replied, 'No, you just have to pick it up as you go along!' God wants us to learn so much as we go along with him.

In this chapter I want to share with you some of the principles of successful Christian living that I have learned over the years.

DON'T LOSE YOUR JOY

We all have the same time-span allotted to us each day. No one is given more time than another. We start off the day at the same place! Here are some words of Arnold Bennett to remind you – and me – how fortunate we are:

> You wake up in the morning and lo! your purse is magically filled with 24 hours of the universe of your life. It is yours. It is the most precious of possessions. No one can take it from you. It is

unstealable and no one receives either more or less than you receive.

Now don't you feel glad to be alive? Many lose their joy in the work of God, their first enthusiasm, and their first love dries up gradually. Don't lose your zip, your peace and your enjoyment of the Christian walk. Never get bored. Enjoy serving Jesus.

BE COURAGEOUS

Christians today need to be courageous people. Now is a time of risk, a time of daring, a time for quiet courage, for dangerous living. God said he would raise up an army of fearless men and women in the last days.

Of all the biblical characters, Caleb is one of the most courageous. He came from the background to the foreground in leadership. He has inspired millions down the ages by his daring spirit. He kept expanding and never fell behind. God kept him strong. To achieve for God, I've found Caleb's courage is irresistible and undeniably vital. You will get nowhere without much courage for God.

Many Christians lose their courage as they grow older. They settle down and lose their cutting edge. We should become more enterprising, bold and fearless with the years – not less!

Oswald Saunders described Caleb as 'the old man who never stopped growing'. His secret was that all through his life he followed the Lord wholeheartedly. The psalmist pictures the man or woman of God as being like a palm tree that brings forth fruit in old age (Psalm 92:19). What was true for Caleb can be true for us all.

I like the story of Gladys Aylward, the missionary to China. No mission board would accept this parlour maid and scrubber of floors as a missionary. Their money was too good for this untalented, simple young woman with little education. But Gladys was not daunted. She knew God had called her to China.

After working hard and saving every penny, Gladys said goodbye to England, and headed across Siberia, on the Trans-Siberian Express, bound for China. Escaping war, rape and near capture by the Communists, she arrived to help an elderly missionary, Jeannie Lawson, in the mountain town of Yangcheng.

No missionary training could have prepared Gladys for the barbaric way of life there. Execution by beheading was a common sight in the market-place.

After a considerable period of being called a 'foreign devil', Gladys became acquainted with the local mandarin. She soon had a band of soldiers escorting her to outlying districts, for she had become the government's foot-inspector! It was Gladys' job to put an end to the custom of 'feet-binding'. As she untied the women's crippled feet and gently flexed the toes into place, Gladys talked about God, the God who lived inside her, and his Son Jesus Christ.

One day there was a great commotion, and Gladys was commanded to go to the town prison, where a riot was in progress and prisoners were killing each other.

'But what do you expect me to do about it?' cried Gladys, wide-eyed.

'You must go in and stop them! You can't be killed, for you said your God lives in you and he'll never die!' explained the prison officers.

Amazed at this theological interpretation of her words, Gladys could not find a suitable answer. She looked down the passage into the prison yard. A tall man with a bloody axe was running after new victims, while the rest of the prisoners were trying to hide from him. Several corpses lay strewn around.

Inwardly trembling, but outwardly courageous, Gladys' little figure marched up to the tall man and demanded the axe.

Glassy-eyed, the man rushed at her, but after a moment he dropped the axe at her feet. Anger and fear were replaced by compassion as Gladys heard the stories of these pitiful men.

That day saw the start of a reform in the prison, for Gladys and 'the God who lived in her' demanded that the appalling conditions should be changed. In addition, this courageous woman brought a line of hand-cuffed prisoners to church every Sunday morning!

Let God increase your courage! Be strong and bold – it works marvels!

GOD IS GOOD TO ME

Many Christians, over the years, tend to lose their wonder at the goodness of God. Like the generation of Israelites in the desert, 'they forget the miracles that their fathers had told them'. The blessings in their lives have become commonplace to them. I find I keep close to God if I constantly remember that God is good to me!

Much of the God-given success which it has been my privilege to witness comes down to this important fact: we cannot repay him, but we can thank him. We must never forget his goodness to us. The psalmist asked, 'How can I repay the Lord for all his goodness to me?' (Psalm 11:12).

When Isobel, a lady living on the island of Ayr, broke

the news that she was expecting a baby, it was sympathy she got, not congratulations. That was because she was 42, with her family grown up and away. She was worried about the risk to babies born to older mothers. But her husband Alec was delighted.

As the months went by, Isobel gradually became used to the idea. When Catriona was born, she and Alec fell into the old routine, making up feeds and changing nappies, but with paper ones rather than the cotton squares she'd used for the rest of the family.

Indeed, Catriona seemed to give them a new lease of life. Then, just after Catriona's ninth birthday, Alec died suddenly. Isobel went through the funeral in a daze. She was only aware of Catriona's hand clutching hers.

And that, says Isobel, is how she has come through the last six years – with Catriona by her side. 'She helped me look to the future instead of the past,' says Isobel, 'and she lifted my spirits when no one else could.'

What's more, she kept the memory of her dad alive more than anyone else, because she never tired of hearing stories about him.

And to think folk thought of her as Isobel's mistake!

Today she is so grateful for that teenage daughter and all the companionship and joy she brings her – she cannot repay God for his goodness to her.

One summer, at the time when 'A' Level students were sitting their exams, I was browsing in a bookshop in Charing Cross Road, thinking about how a piece of paper can make all the difference between being accepted for a university place and being turned down.

It reminded me of two teenage boys at the turn of the century who failed their exams. They decided to sell the text-books they no longer needed, and so they advertised them in a newspaper.

They received scores of replies. But instead of selling to the first bidder, they thought of a better idea. They scoured the second-hand bookshops for other copies of the books they had offered for sale. They filled all the requests and made a fair profit.

More importantly, they saw an opening. By working 15 hours a day they built up a business in second-hand books. Before many years had passed, William and Gilbert Foyle owned the biggest bookshop in London, the very shop I was browsing in.

Success is often failure turned inside out. What seemed like an awful start to life turned out to be the way to prosperity and a great future. They could hardly repay God for his goodness to them.

We are reminded in 2 Chronicles 16:12 to 'Remember the wonders he has done, his miracles, and the judgements he pronounced.' David advised, 'Sing to him, sing praises to him, tell of all his wonderful acts' (1 Chronicles 16:9). We cannot repay God – we can only tell him we are grateful.

God meets all our needs – he is always there to help. God is good. Gird yourself with thanksgiving. Gratitude is a spiritual attitude. 'In everything give thanks, for this is the will of God in Christ Jesus concerning you' (1 Thessalonians 5:18).

Out of the blue you are shown a great favour. Taken by surprise, you say, 'What have I done to deserve this?' You are embarrassed by such kindness; you do not know what to do in return for being treated so well.

The man who wrote Psalm 116 felt like that. He was embarrassed by the goodness of God to him, and so he asked the question: 'How can I repay the Lord for all his goodness to me?'

Psalm 116 has just one theme: it focuses on the

loving goodness of God. 'I love the Lord' is the first note, and all the rest says in effect: 'God is good to me.'

Not that life had been easy for the psalmist; just the reverse. The path for him was rough and steep, he had been finding it very hard going.

In his *Pilgrim's Progress*, John Bunyan tells of a similar experience when Christian has to climb Hill Difficulty. 'I looked, then, after Christian, to see him go up the hill, where I perceived he fell from running to going, and from going to clambering on his hands and knees, because of the steepness of the place.'

A quick glance through the psalmist's song will give us some idea of the hill he'd had to climb. Verse 3 says the most about it: 'The cords of death entangled me, the anguish of the grave came over me; I was overcome by trouble and sorrow.'

We cannot be sure what particular distress he had gone through. It could be that he had had a close brush with death, or that a loved one had been near to death.

On the other hand, it may be referring to some agony of mind, some despair with no apparent light at the end of the tunnel, some spiritual battle in which all hell seemed to be let loose against his soul.

Whatever the trouble and sorrow he had been through, it had threatened to engulf him. Looking back, he speaks of having been in 'great need' (verse 6), of 'tears' and the danger of 'stumbling' (verse 8) and of having been 'greatly afflicted' (verse 10).

Twice he uses the word 'death' to describe the trauma he had come through: 'The cords of death entangled me' (verse 3); 'you, O Lord, have delivered my soul from death' (verse 8).

Life had not been a bed of roses for him, not by any means, yet he did not whimper or whine, nor did he wrap himself up into a little parcel of self-pity.

Clambering on his hands and knees because of the steepness of his Hill Difficulty, he had cried out to God. His prayers had been like emergency telegrams to heaven: 'O Lord, save me!' (verse 4). And God had done just that; he had delivered his soul (verse 8).

Now that the man is on safe, level ground again, he praises the Lord with this Hallel Psalm: 'I love the Lord, because he heard my voice; he heard my cry for mercy' (verse 1). He feels that God has been so good to him in hearing him and saving him. It is then that he asks his question: 'How can I repay the Lord for all his goodness to me?' He is embarassed by the goodness of God.

The goodness of God is most clearly expressed in the character and life of his Son, Jesus Christ. Christ went about doing good every day; from morning until night, he sought those who were lost. Worn out one day, he sat by the well at Sychar – and won another soul! Dog tired, he fell asleep in the stern of a boat on another occasion. On yet another day he had to go into the mountains to rest awhile.

His days were full of errands of mercy: healing the sick, blessing the children and families, comforting the bereaved and raising their dead! He did many errands of emancipation: he set captives free, he broke people's demonic bondages, he made the possessed sane again.

There was scarcely a village in the whole country that he did not visit: 'I must go on to the next town . . . I must steadfastly set my face to go to Jerusalem,' he cried. Foxes had holes, birds of the air had nests, but the Son of man had nowhere to lay his head. His body only rested when it lay in the tomb for three days.

What touching sympathy Christ imparted. He made personal contact. He touched the leper, he anointed the blind, he released the ears of the deaf, he made available the hem of his garment – as many as touched it were made perfectly whole. How good he is!

The psalmist, in his response to God's goodness, says: 'I will lift up the cup of salvation, and call on the name of the Lord; I will fulfil my vows to the Lord in the presence of all his people.' It seems to be not much of a repayment! But, that is exactly the point. He owns 'the cattle on a thousand hills' (Psalm 50:10), so we cannot repay God – we can only tell him we are grateful. Showing our gratitude – that is the gist of this psalm.

The psalm shows us three ways in which we can tell God that we are grateful. First, we should lift up the cup of salvation. This was actually a custom of the times. When a Jewish family had come through some crisis and had realized that God had intervened in the situation to deliver them, they would perform a simple ceremony. At a family meal, the father would take a cup of wine in his hands and would recount to all the household the story of what had happened and how God had helped them. Then they would drink together from that 'cup of deliverance'.

Whatever the crisis in our life, we should go over the story and thank God for rescuing us. The greatest deliverance we will ever know is the salvation from sin and death and hell that we have in Christ. We cannot repay God for that; it costs too much. But we can lift up our cup of salvation.

If Christ has cleansed us from our sins, we should enjoy his forgiveness; if Christ has delivered us from the dominion of darkness, we should stand firm in our liberty; if Christ has reconciled us to God, we should live as people who are really at peace with God.

We have been reconciled to God through the death of

his Son. Give thanks. 'Christ hath purged us from our sins and sat down at the right hand of the Father . . .'

That old fence! It was a real problem to two neighbours named Bill and Tom. They went to the same place of worship but never talked for years. When Bill had erected it, Tom had accused him of taking two inches of his land. Bill denied it, and they had nearly come to blows! Then a revival broke out in their church; they were almost the last to repent. The next day, Bill sheepishly knocked on his neighbour's door and asked to see him. He entered and offered to read a scripture. Tom, when his turn came, could not find his glasses, so Bill loaned him his. As Tom read Psalm 27, he added, 'That old fence looks different through your glasses, Bill!' Everything looks different when we are reconciled and have drank his cup of salvation.

Secondly, we should call on the name of the Lord. We call on the name of the Lord when we trust him. So the psalmist is saying that one way of showing gratitude to God for his goodness is to trust him to be good to us again! We need his help in so many ways; ultimately, without him we can do nothing. God is honoured by his people when they depend on him for everything.

We also call on the name of the Lord when we worship him. There is a lot of talk about worship today. We compare worship songs and contrast worship styles; we attend worship seminars led by worship specialists! We discuss 'how to make worship an enjoyable experience' and 'how to get the most out of worship'. We are in danger of worshipping worship. The whole thing has become subjective and man-centred. Isn't worship for God – not for us?

Whether we engage in the current debate or merely

keep on in our own chosen way, the fact is that worship is our highest duty and we are not very good at it. Would we not do better if we valued our salvation more? Those who know they are forgiven the most, love the most (see Luke 7:47).

In Sicily in 1943, a soldier was burying all his friends after the great battle there. They had come through many months together and many such confrontations with the enemy. But now only he was left. He felt that his faith in God had gone. 'Can I believe anymore?' he asked himself.

Then, returning from the makeshift graveyard alone, he stumbled and fell into a shell-hole. As he lay there, a miracle happened which gave birth to fresh hope. In the darkness of the hole, in the midst of the mud, blood and blackness, he saw the tiny shoot of a flower – it was pushing its way through.

It was a sign of new creation, life springing up into the light. He rose and went his way, making a new vow to God. Calling on the name of the Lord again, he had joy amidst despair, for God's power conquers darkness. He follows Christ to this day, and never forgets that moment of gratitude, as he learnt of the goodness of God in the middle of a battlefield!

Thirdly, we should fulfil our vows to the Lord. It is likely that, in his time of great need, the man who was later to become embarrassed by the goodness of God made a promise to God. Maybe as he climbed the hill and cried to the Lord to save him, he prayed: 'Lord, if you will help me, I promise that I will live for you for the rest of my life.' Now that he was over the hump of his trouble, he was determined to keep his promise and fulfil his vow.

Sadly, it must be said that some who make hurried

promises to God in times of crisis do not keep those promises afterwards. The Bible says: 'It is better not to vow than to make a vow and not fulful it' (Ecclesiastes 5:5).

The fact is that every believer is under vows to Christ, for he is our Master and our Lord. We are his servants; he has freed us from our chains. We are 'not our own', we are 'bought with a price' (2 Corinthians 6:19-20).

God has been good to us and he is good to us. Let's honour him and let's honour our vows. We must put our lives at his disposal so that his glorious name will be renowned throughout our society.

God honours those who honour him. Those who keep their vows have the door of miracles open to them!

LIVE PEACEABLY

Another important principle of Christian living is to learn to live peaceably. Seek to keep peace both in your heart and with others. With peace you're rich. You can be penniless financially, but spiritually richer than a millionaire. Get peace, and you have a wonderful life.

An art competition was once held, and the painters had to produce pictures on the subject of peace. One of the two finalists depicted a marvellous, serene, still ocean: there were no people, no birds, just blue sky, quiet and calm. But the other artist pipped him at the post and won the great prize. His picture showed pouring rain, a dark, dismal sky, lightning piercing the blackness and fierce gales. But in the corner of the masterpiece, was a small bird's nest in the cleft of a rock. The chicks in the nest looked contented, sheltered from the storm, looking up into mother's eyes. She stood over them, singing a bright song, unmoved by the storm! That was the artist's idea of peace.

For peace is not having everything all beautiful and good, and calm and easy. Peace is to live in this world of turbulence, uncertainty, sickness, trial, adversity, problems, battles, temptations, stresses and anxieties, and yet to be free. Peace is not to escape from the world: it is to be in the world and yet not dominated by it. If we have peace, there will be no storms inside us, whatever is happening around us. Learn to stay where peace is. Stay close to the Saviour. As someone once said, 'Keep peace – don't go to pieces!'

When I was leading a gospel campaign in Hawaii, I noted a huge and unusual statue of Jesus. He was coming in from an all-night vigil in the mountains, looking for the lost sheep. He was cold, his beard was ragged, rain-drops flowed down his face, and he looked very tired. He had been up all night amidst great dangers, struggling through the storm to find the tiny, cold lamb. By contrast, the lamb lay peacefully on his chest, looking safe, happy and contented – saved. It was a remarkable sculpture of the suffering Christ, who went out to bring us to safety, assurance and peace! Christ bought us peace by the blood of his cross. It cost him everything.

LET PRESSURE OPEN THE DOOR

It is important that we let the pressure in our lives open the door to God for us. It's a hard, heartbroken world, full of pressures of various kinds. But some times of intense pressure can help us look beyond ourselves and put our trust in God. Such situations reduce our selfishness and increase our teachability.

God is not tied to our time schedules. He will deliver us from circumstances that threaten to crush us, but not before we have learned the lessons he wants to teach us.

After the Israelites had crossed the Red Sea, they sang as they had never done before. What a choir it must have been, with its many thousands of voices! The theme of their song was the Lord. Moses was not even mentioned! The song was sung to the Lord and about the Lord. All the honours of victory were reverently laid at his feet. Moses would not have wanted it any other way.

Cheer up Christian! Despite all the Red Seas of your experience, you too will yet sing as Israel did. Between the devil and your deep Red Sea you will discover that weeping endures for a night, but joy comes in the morning. You just wait and see!

I am often pressed in by extreme pressures. I work in dozens of missions yearly in towns, villages and cities. I am travelling constantly, often held up in traffic jams, and occasionally by fog or late planes. Sometimes I have to sleep in caravans or on the back seats of cars, or on all-night trains and boats. I am asked to pray for many thousands of sick people annually. I often have to face a critical and cynical press. I write two paperback books each year. I lead missions in the hardest spots on earth, including the Falklands, IRA towns, difficult areas of Europe like Belgium and Austria, and even the outback of Australia. I also have to manage the mission's finances with no denominational support from Bishops, church leaders or ecclesiastical headquarters.

But I find that God can turn all the demands and pressures in to an open door to greater spiritual realities and blessings. In all these stresses, after a while, I have to turn away in my imagination to that lonely, twisted, tortured figure on the cross, nails through his hands and feet, his back lacerated, his limbs wrenched, his brow bleeding from thorn prickles, his throat intolerably dry, plunged in God-forsaken darkness.

That is the God for me! Our sufferings become more manageable in the light of his. There is still a question mark against human suffering, but over it we boldly stamp another mark – the cross which symbolizes divine suffering. The cross of Christ is God's only self-justification.

A famous wrestler once said there is only one thing to do when your opponent has got you in a double Nelson: 'Don't fight too hard against it; your enemy will only tighten his grip. Go with the hold, give yourself time, baffle your opponent, till you can work out your next move. Soon he relaxes, as he cannot grip for too long. That gives you the moment and strength to counter-attack and break out!'

The devil sometimes has us cornered with trials and difficulties. The situation seems impossible and we feel overwhelmed by fear and despair. The answer is, don't fight hard against it; take time to think it out and pray it through. Let the pressure open the door to a closer experience of God; let him teach you through it.

Then the break-through comes, the miracle happens, the door opens, the problem is resolved. Don't struggle against your troubles. Let God speak to you through them.

BECOME A SERVANT

Another principle for success in God is to become a servant. Say, 'I'm glad to serve.' A key to winning hard-bitten materialists is to love them, to show kindness to them, to serve them! As we seek to serve and are concerned about people, we become indispensable.

Mary McInnes is the youngest and only surviving member of a family of five, and at 86 her thoughts often turn to the past. When I visited her one day in November I found her in a sombre mood. It was the time of year, she explained. Not the season with its bonny gold and russet shades, but because the nation would be remembering those who had died in battle. It never failed to move her.

She had been looking at her earliest photo albums and had come across photographs of her three brothers and several cousins, all of whom were amongst the fallen in the First World War. Wearing their uniforms with apparent pride, they gazed unseeingly from the faded photographs Mary showed me.

'You must have so many memories,' I said. 'Such fine-looking men.'

'Aye,' she replied, 'fine-looking, but as my mother used to say, they were just laddies . . .' Her voice faded away as she fumbled for her handkerchief.

Just laddies. And there were tens of thousands like them whose young lives should have been full of opportunity. There were many sorrowing parents, too, such as Mary's mother. We do well to remember, and to be moved by their sacrifice.

This is the greatest service of all. I have seen some of the famous battlefields of the world when I have been on mission travels. I have stood on the sites where millions fell, such as the Somme, Mons, Waterloo, Arnhem, Dunkirk and Singapore. I have read on stones, huge memorials and plaques the soldier's most notable text from Holy Scripture: 'Greater love hath no man than this, that a man lay down his life for his friends.'

Our service today may be much less sacrificial, but it is important to our troubled times; we must serve the lonely, sad, bereaved people of the world.

The pantomime season brings laughter to children and grown-ups alike all over the country. Sister Marie had spent her life working in children's homes. She remembers that several years ago 36 youngsters enjoyed a visit to the theatre to see *Cinderella*. They talked about it excitedly afterwards, except for Joanne and Suzanne, aged eleven and twelve, who were very quiet.

A few nights later, on a cold, wet evening, the back door-bell rang. The Sister on duty found a stranger on the doorstep, wearing an overcoat, a flat cap and a muffler. When he stepped inside, she was amazed to find it was the famous actor, Harry Corbett, from the TV series *Steptoe and Son*.

He smiled and explained that Joanne and Suzanne had written to him after seeing him in the pantomime, asking him to supper. So on his one free evening, Harry had come in person. It was a magical evening for the youngsters. He told them stories, played games with them, and signed autographs.

Sadly, Harry Corbett died a comparatively young man. Most people remember him as a great character actor. Sister Marie has a more special memory of the man in the muffler who appeared out of the rain to give 36 children in care an evening they would never forget. May we love children and have a serving heart like this!

A preacher friend of mine had a test recently which proved he has a servant's heart. He is very busy, travelling all over the UK and Europe on tight schedules, ministering and teaching, plus running one of Britain's largest Christian fellowships, but he is still a servant at heart. He writes:

> I was standing in the courtyard of our home in Esher, Surrey, when I heard a loud bang. I walked out to the pathway of our road, expecting to see a car crash, but it was a break-in over the road.
>
> I called the police and arrests were made amid blue lights, blocked-off roads and a massive dose of adrenalin.
>
> The owners of the house were away at an evening engagement and returned to find the house surrounded by police, dogs and frenetic activity.
>
> We explained the situation and, as their front door was smashed in, invited them back to our house for supper and drinks and to stay the night.
>
> Since then, they have regarded us as 'the best neighbours we have ever known'. The fact is, we are probably the only neighbours they ever had!

We are called to follow the example of Jesus. He became a servant. Paul reminds us, 'He made himself of no reputation . . . He took upon him the form of a servant, and was made in the likeness of men . . .' (Philippians 2:7). J. B. Phillips translates the same verse thus: 'He laid aside his reputation and came and stood by us . . .' Paul says, 'Your attitude should be the same as that of Christ Jesus' (verse 5).

'If a seed die in the ground it shall be raised up again . . .' Dying to the self life and living for others brings new blessings and freedoms. Jesus Christ was and is the creator and sustainer, the Lord of all there is and ever shall be. Yet this Jesus 'made himself nothing'. He laid aside his divine glory as the Son of God and became the child of a carpenter in the village of Nazareth.

He suffered the attacks of conceited, powerful men, and the failure of dear friends to stay with him when he needed them. He touched lepers, washed dirty feet, allowed rough soldiers to beat him and nail him to a cross, and he entered the darkness of death.

Why, oh why, did he do it? Because these actions add up to true life for the Son of God. They speak of humility, service, sacrifice: he never grasped for his rights but always counted the needs of others as more important than his own comfort and safety.

So the Christian must ask: Can there ever be a situation or a time when I, who try to walk in his way, can justly stand up for my rights? I cannot make any claims to rights where God is concerned. He is the judge of everyone, and I stand before him as a sinner. My disobedience, my flaunting of the Creator's laws, declare that I am under judgement.

Nor can I claim 'my rights' in dealing with my fellow men and women, for I am called to follow the example of Jesus – to wash feet, to go the extra mile, even to love my enemy, to be willing to give my life that he might live, to share in Christ's sufferings.

In Paul's own words, there must be no 'selfish ambition or vain conceit' in my life. There is no room for 'complaining or arguing'. And I have to work this out in practice in my daily relationships with my wife, my children, my neighbours.

It shouldn't be arguments with other people that get me worked up – but opportunities to serve, to show compassion, to encourage and lift up others.

So often, I find myself turning to the example of Barnabas in the Acts of the Apostles. It was Barnabas who brought Saul (later Paul) to the disciples at Antioch, who gave John Mark a second chance, who took second place to Paul in the ministry.

He never demanded his rights, but always put the work of God and the encouragement and building up of others before his own pleasure. Oh, to be a Barnabas – an encourager, a servant, a blessing and a joy to all those we meet! I have never known a great Christian who was not a great servant.

BE DILIGENT

We cannot go forward in the Christian life without diligence. I have seen so many Christians get enthusiastic about the things of God, and then grow cold in their faith. I remember one young brother in a town in Wiltshire, who hoped to do great things for God. His church had held a series of packed meetings in the Town Hall, and God gave us some outstanding miracles of healing. For a year or two afterwards the church had a large membership.

Then I was away crusading for several months, and on my return I went along to encourage him. I noticed that he gave me no welcome and never referred to the healing meetings. His wife acted in the same strange way. I was away again for some time, and when I visited the church again I saw that the congregation had shrunk greatly; even some of the good, solid elders had 'gone to other churches'.

I sought out the young man to chat with him. It seemed that a spirit of arrogance had crept in to his life.

He said he didn't need any help or advice.

The work of that church almost petered out. Many of the people wandered away from church involvement. Fortunately a new church started up in a neighbouring town, and many of the wandering people joined it. It now thrives, with large numbers attending.

What was it that virtually destroyed the faith of such a fine fellow? It was a lack of diligence. He started breaking his word to people; he said, 'I will do so and so,' and yet we are still waiting for him to do it! He became gradually untrustworthy, he did not watch over his soul, he would not let mature Christians watch over him and guide him. He failed in diligence. During nearly 40 years in the ministry, I have seen many cases like that.

We must have a goal, an aim. God's people had this right from the beginning of time. God told Adam and Eve to 'Subdue the earth and have dominion over it' (Genesis 1:28). Through turning away from the Creator, man has become self-centred and self-serving. God's Kingdom-children must see with clarity the goals which God has designed for them. Diligence is vital if we are to have the power of Almighty God in our lives.

Diligence is not necessarily the same thing as being busy. In Luke chapter 10 we read that Martha was working hard, but Jesus told her that her sister Mary, who was just sitting at his feet, listening to him, had got her priorities right. Bernard of Clairvaux said, 'Waiting on God is work which beats all other work.' Diligence is an outward attitude which springs from a deep desire for an intimate relationship with God. This kind of inward longing to know God more never stops. Many become starved and stagnant because this diligence is not followed.

171

God gives us assignments and goals based on his knowledge of us. His wisdom, ways, guidance and instructions are best. He never asks anything of us that could not, by divine help and the capacity in us, be realistically achieved.

We must not let this possibility lie dormant. In Matthew chapter 25 we see the third servant let his talent come to nothing. He had a total misunderstanding within his heart. He said, 'Lord, I know thee, that thou art a hard man . . .' He did not know God truly, he did not love him as he should have, he did not have a right concept of him.

God is loving, not hard; he is good, and he wants to bless us and do us good. We must know the character of God. He is faithful, reliable, willing to answer, waiting to bless and change us.

This young man in Wiltshire was afraid to invest, afraid he might fail, afraid to take a risk. Tozer said, 'God works as long as his people live daringly. He ceases when they no longer need his aid.'

When Jesus asked him what he wanted, blind Bartimaeus replied, 'Lord, that I may receive my sight!' (Mark 10:51). He was *bold* in asking Jesus for what he wanted.

Scripture promises, 'The soul of the diligent shall be made fat, the soul of the sluggard shall have nothing' (Proverbs 13:4) and 'The thoughts of the diligent tend only to plenteousness' (Proverbs 21:5).

There are three steps to keeping diligence: (1) Build strong foundations in your life on God's word; (2) Progress a step at a time, with patience and persistence (see Romans 4:12); (3) Set your standards high and dare to expect God's best.

Obedience to God is part of diligence. Obeying God

sets the stage for great things to happen. In John's Gospel Jesus told the blind man, 'Go to the pool of Siloam and wash,' and he did as he was told and so received his sight (John 9:11). Delayed obedience brings delayed results.

SEEK WISDOM

We need to weep over so many of our churches. That smell of death, little expectancy, lack of wisdom, staleness, emptiness, doubt and hopelessness pervades them. The Kingdom of Jesus is very different to this: it is a Kingdom of light, guidance, victory, hope, gladness, joy, peace, expansion and success.

Wisdom is not an option but a requirement for a triumphant church. To have God's wisdom is to enter the heart of God. Paul prayed for the Colossian believers, 'I do not cease to pray for you, and to ask that you may be filled with . . . all wisdom and spiritual understanding . . . fully pleasing him, being fruitful in every good work, and increasing in the Kingdom of God' (Colossians 1:9-10). Scripture says, 'For the Lord gives wisdom, for he stores up wisdom for the upright' (Proverbs 2:6-7).

The best news is that God wants to share his wisdom with us more than we want to receive it. Sometimes I used to go blustering and pushing my way into a town without asking my Father about it, and all sorts of problems would arise. I have learned to wait for God's wisdom before rushing into a situation. What a difference that makes! Wisdom is the vehicle for getting you to the place you need to go.

15

A THREE-FOLD FAITH

Luke's account of the conversion of the Ethiopian eunuch in Acts 8 tells us some important things about the Christian faith. Luke first of all reminds us of the necessary qualification for any evangelist: a listening ear and a ready will.

An 'angel of the Lord' spoke to Philip, and 'he started out' (verses 26-27). No true evangelist puts up his tent or decides upon his sphere of evangelistic operation until he has received divine directions.

Philip immediately left Jerusalem for Gaza, taking the route indicated to him – 'the desert road'. On his way he met an Ethiopian eunuch. Now this man was 'an important official'. He had 'charge of all the treasury of Candace, queen of the Ethiopians'. In other words, he was her chancellor of the exchequer. Jesus called both manual workers and professional people, blue-collar and white-collar workers.

This chancellor of the exchequer was a religious man. He had 'gone to Jerusalem to worship', but he did not know Jesus as his own personal Saviour. He was reading the book of Isaiah on his way home from the religious festival in Jerusalem, but he could not understand what he was reading.

Once again, Philip was the true evangelist. This time he heard not the voice of an angel of the Lord but that of 'the Spirit' (verse 29). The Holy Spirit told Philip to approach the chariot and 'stay near it' (verse 29).

So, Christians should listen to the voice of the Spirit each morning, telling us whom we should approach and get alongside that particular day, either at school or college, in the office or factory, in a neighbour's home or at the supermarket checkout.

There was no beating about the bush with Philip. He went straight in: 'Do you understand what you are reading?' he asked. It was the practice in those days to read aloud, so Philip heard what the Ethiopian was reading from the book of Isaiah.

Luke records only that he had been reading Isaiah 53:7-8. Before that, he must have read these words: 'He was pierced for our transgressions, he was crushed for our iniquities . . . the Lord has laid on him the iniquity of us all' (verses 5-6).

What an opportunity for Philip! How he must have revelled in preaching the substitutionary death of the Lord Jesus Christ, telling the Ethiopian how Jesus took our sins, our punishment and our guilt, when he died at Calvary!

The Ethiopian eunuch, as a religious person, must have known about baptism, for he then asked Philip, 'Why shouldn't I be baptised?' (Acts 8:37).

The conversion of the Ethiopian shows us that Christian faith is a three-fold faith.

PERSONAL FAITH

First, the Ethiopian had to have personal faith. There is nothing about 'piggy-back' Christians in the Bible. We cannot get to heaven on the back of someone else's faith. It is no good saying at the gate of heaven: 'My father was a minister of the gospel' or 'My parents were missionaries.' It will be no use claiming that we were brought up in a Christian home and that father was an elder or a deacon. However godly our parents may have been, our faith must be our own.

A man once said to me, 'I'm not a Christian, but my wife is. I don't go to church – she goes for me.' But, you know, she cannot go for you; she cannot get faith for you; the priest cannot do it for you; Mary, the Pope, Billy Graham and the Vicar cannot do it for you!

One lady with a posh Oxford accent once said to me, 'I was born in a manse, and my father was a very good minister, so I ought to be a Christian.' But her father could not do it for her.

Personal faith is vital. God wants us to have a loving, earnest, seeking, personal belief. 'One of life's thrills for my wife and me came a few years ago, before our son died of cancer,' says a minister. He was speaking in the open air at the Keswick in Wales Convention in Llandrindod Wells, and we listened over the amplification system in a nearby street, as he didn't want to see us in the crowd standing around him. He began by saying, 'I am not going to tell you about my father's faith, I am going to tell you about my own personal faith in Christ. He is now in heaven, but he did not get there by me giving him a piggy-back.'

POSSESSIVE FAITH

God wants us to believe in him with all our heart, to have a possessive faith. Some people want to believe with a part of their heart only. For example, they claim to be Christians but they still want to read their horoscope in the daily newspaper!

Far too many churches are satisfied with a low level of faith. They are grateful for a small yearly increase in membership; they are not interested in revival – indeed, they are frightened of it! So they are missing what the Lord is doing in these days.

We cannot believe in the certainties of the gospel and also in the chance jottings of the fortune-teller or the astrologer. I have known Christians who may say to a friend taking a driving test, 'I'll keep my fingers crossed for you,' instead of saying, 'I'll pray for you.' One man tried to Christianize this remark by saying, 'I'll keep my spiritual fingers crossed for you.' Yet another said: 'I'm going to the doctor for a check-up; touch wood, he'll find nothing wrong with me.'

It is only part-belief and not possessive faith when a Christian will not walk beneath a ladder, put up an umbrella indoors, or thinks it unlucky to break a mirror. We must reject all superstition and fully embrace the gospel of freedom in Christ.

The Ethiopian embraced the gospel without reservation: his was a possessive faith.

PERCEPTIBLE FAITH

There was a third quality to the faith of the Ethiopian. It was a perceptible faith, a faith that could be seen by others. He was now dead to sin, his sins were drowned in the deepest sea, and he was walking in the newness of life.

Where were the onlookers of such perceptible faith? In the desert, water can be found at an oasis. Travellers gathered at an oasis. There was also his chariot driver, for this important official would have been chauffeur-driven. No way could he drive himself and read from a heavy Scripture scroll at the same time! He may also have been accompanied by servants and guards.

So in the presence of the travellers and his own retinue he was baptized by Philip. He was prepared to stand up and be counted as a Christian. When I was a boy at Sunday School we used to sing, 'Stand up, stand up for Jesus, Ye soldiers of the Cross . . .' Christians today need to stand up for the true, pure good news of the gospel. In our generation faith is being revived. People are once again standing up and sharing the perceptible faith.

Yes, the Ethiopian's faith was very perceptible: he had 'nailed his colours to the mast'. No wonder he 'went on his way rejoicing' (Acts 8:39). Joy always fills the heart of the believer who is prepared to confess with his lips as well as believe with his heart. By his baptism this man had publicly declared his belief that Jesus Christ is the Son of God.

We must make a stand for Christ. Our world is being swept away by wickedness, despair, worldliness, wrong directions and permissiveness. We must walk in the light, shine out for Jesus, pray, work and shake whole towns and cities, to win thousands of non-churchgoing people. We must take the naked Word, with faith and love to whole communities.

We must pray the prayer of a friend of mine who is a Baptist pastor: 'Lord God, heavenly Father, I do believe; help me overcome my unbelief. Help me to believe personally, possessively, and perceptibly, believing with all my heart. Enable me by your Holy Spirit to confess you before others at all times. May my joy so increase and abound that it may help others to believe and also bring glory to your holy name. Amen.'

God is calling us all to repeat Philip's work in our generation.

16

GOD'S LOVE FOR US

Each of us is only a number today. For the purposes of Income Tax or National Insurance and many other things, we are referred to by a mere string of digits. Man has lost his identity. The world does not care; it is hard and feelingless. People are lonely and have lost their way. But, in contrast to the lovelessness of modern human society, God loves us more than we can possibly imagine. 'How great is the love the father has lavished on us, that we should be called children of God! And that is what we are!' (1 John 3:1).

To God we are not a number. He cares for us, loves us and watches over us. People today are in desperate need. We receive hundreds of phone calls at our mission office from people in trouble. Sometimes they even break down in tears and sob on the phone. God does not leave us struggling without answers!

When God gave us Jesus Christ, he gave himself. Let's ponder on this love which has been the motivating force behind every blessing, conversion, healing and act of God that I have ever witnessed.

When words of love are first addressed to us, we are invariably moved. How much more wonderful it is when, as the Holy Spirit applies God's Word to our souls, we hear God say, 'I love you.'

The Father's love is a gift. It is something that he has lavished on us, and we don't deserve it at all. There never was and there never could be anything in us to attract God's love, since we deserve his condemnation for our sinful disobedience and rebellion against him.

It is an observable fact that God has not chosen to lavish his love upon the best of men and women, but more often upon the worst of sinners. He has loved us because he intended to love us. The supreme illustration of his lavish and unmerited love is the gift of his Son, our Lord Jesus Christ – the gift of gifts.

In fact, everything depends upon God. His love towards us never diminishes. Our sins may certainly hinder our awareness of his love, and the fruits of it, but they do not cause God's love for us as his children to cease. God rebukes, but his love does not change.

The expression in 1 John 3:1 which is translated 'How great is . . .' means literally 'of what country' and conveys a sense of astonishment. John is saying that God's love is 'out of this world'.

When we think of who it is that God loves, that love seems almost incredible. We tend to love only the deserving; God loves the undeserving. We are inclined to love the attractive; God loves the unattractive.

For the Father, therefore, to permit – and even cause – his Son to be made sin for us is a truth which the angels continue to marvel at – as we ourselves shall continue to do throughout eternity.

The direct consequence of Calvary is that Christians can be called the sons and daughters of God. New birth means adoption into God's family, although by nature we belong to a very different family.

God takes a family for himself out of Satan's kingdom, and adopts it as his own children. He gives us even more than the name of sons and daughters, for he gives us his spirit, so that we may participate in the divine nature, so that we really are his children.

The world at large may be unaware of what has happened to us, but the whole of creation is on tiptoe to see the wonderful sight of God's children coming into their own when our Lord Jesus Christ returns.

If we are sons and daughters of God, then we are heirs. In fact, we are joint-heirs with our Lord Jesus Christ. We are to share in all that is his: his throne, his kingdom and his glory. We are 'in Christ', and the Father loves us with the love with which he loves his son.

Various translators have wrestled with 1 John 3:1. For example: 'Consider the incredible love that the Father has shown us in allowing us to be called 'children of God' (J. B. Phillips); 'Think what love the Father has for us, in letting us be called "children of God" ' (Moffatt); 'See how much the Father has loved us! His love is so great that we are called God's children – and so, in fact, we are' (Good News Bible).

We must believe in the love the Father has for us. As we meditate on God's love, we know ourselves to be secure in it. Viewing it, we say to ourselves: 'If God is for us, who can be against us?' God's love is the sure rest for our soul.

As we view God's love, we love him in return. The Father's love is an antecedent or preceding love. Our love for him is a consequent love. As we consider his love, we feel the constraint which it places upon us to obey him. How can we not want to obey the God who loves us so? We find ourselves wanting to give ourselves to him.

We must give time to pondering the unfailing character of God's love especially when we are tested. God is always loving us with the same intensity as when our Lord Jesus died for us. His love is like an inexhaustible fountain. As we sit beside it, we quickly discover afresh how sweet are its waters, and the inestimable refreshment it brings to our soul and life. Nothing can replace, in a Christian's life, the benefits of pondering the Father's love! We should meditate until we adore! *Remember the love of God!*

17

GOD IN OUR SUFFERING

The well-known German theologian, Helmut Thielike, was recently asked what was the greatest deficiency of the churches in the West today. He replied, 'They have an inadequate view of suffering.'

God wants us to master the storms and tests of life. He wants us to be triumphant, not tormented. Through Jesus Christ he has given us the victory over suffering.

Paul could say about his own suffering, 'Now I want you to know, brothers, that what has happened to me has really served to advance the gospel' (Philippians 1:12). Some are soured and some are sweetened by challenge and hardships.

God can reveal to us his goodness in the storms. He can keep us steady as a rock in these tense times. Many Christians think only good can ever happen to them. They think they will never face any battles, losses, heartaches or trials. God is all-powerful, but that does not mean that he necessarily protects us from every evil, temptation, struggle or hardship in life. Life is going to be a battle, a fight and a challenge if it is to mean anything.

Paul suffered dreadfully at times, but he was able to proclaim, 'We know that in all things God works for the good of those who love him' (Romans 8:28). Philip Yancey wrote a book entitled *Where is God when it hurts?* The answer I give to that is, *RIGHT BESIDE YOU, HELPING YOU THROUGH!* He gives us 'the garment of praise, instead of a spirit of despair' (Isaiah 6:3). 'Weeping may remain for a night, but rejoicing comes in the morning' (Psalm 30:5). Augustine said, 'A greater joy is always preceded by a greater suffering.' George Wald, the Nobel Prize winner, said, 'When you have no experience of pain, it is hard to experience joy in life.'

Suffering is not something we should try to avoid but something we ought to embrace. It whets our appetite for eternity, moves us forward in the direction of heaven, quickens our footsteps toward home, and enables us to walk through this sin-stained world with hope.

In *God in the Dock* C. S. Lewis put it like this:

> Imagine a set of people living in the same building. Half of them think it is an hotel, the other half think it is a prison. Those who think it is an hotel regard it as quite intolerable and those who thought it was a prison might decide it was surprisingly comfortable. So it seems the ugly doctrine is one that comforts you in the end.

Paul Tournier wrote a book called *Creative Suffering*. In it he mentions 300 famous people who have done good to the world. All were orphans and had it very rough in their early life. Leo Tolstoy said it was 'by those who have suffered that the world has been advanced'.

God is good, he changes not. All his ways are best for us. Even through trials and disturbances he is dependable and never fails us. Faith gives us enduring power through all of life's demands, hardships, heartbreaks, gales and shakings. No storm can sink the ship in which

Christ is riding. When the disciples cried out, 'Master, Master, we're going to drown!' Jesus got up and rebuked the wind and waves, and the storm subsided (Luke 8:24).

God is totally reliable. Through him we always triumph. 'Thanks be to God, who always leads us in triumphal procession in Christ' (2 Corinthians 2:14). We cannot avoid adversity, but we can, with God's help, seek to use it.

'The people exhaust themselves for nothing' (Jeremiah 51:58). That is the result of worry, complaining and fighting bitterly against our hardships and adversities. Paul had a very different attitude: 'For Christ's sake I delight in weaknesses, in insults, hardships, persecutions, in difficulties, for when I am weak, then I am made strong' (2 Corinthians 12:10).

Perhaps you have heard of the stone fence that was as wide as it was high, so that when it blew over, it was as high as it was before! The Christian who has the right mind-set and the right attitudes is like that. He or she thrives on difficulties, turning them into doors through which they walk into a new understanding of life and of God.

Are you being criticized at the moment? If the criticism is true, correct the thing that is being criticized. Make your critics the 'unpaid watchmen of your soul'.

The trials and suffering of this life will not last for ever. Teresa of Avila wrote, 'From heaven the most miserable life will look like one bad night in an inconvenient hotel.' Paul said, 'The troubles of this present time are nothing to be compared with the glory we shall share.'

God wants us to get through life, to win, to bear fruit, to overcome, to live a godly life, to leave the world

185

better than we found it, to learn from all our struggles, heartaches, fights, sloggings, stresses, adversities and turbulences, so that we will be better, sweeter, more loving people, leaving joy and blessing behind for the next generation.

Two women in a church suffered the same affliction. One became a bitter person; the other became a better person. The first one allowed it to drag her down into despair. The second emerged from it triumphantly. The difference was that the second woman was adjusted to God and his will and purposes for her life; the other was not. The same circumstances; two different results.

The raw materials of human life, the things that come on us day by day, can be woven into garments of character. All of this, of course, depends on the attitude we take.

I love this story concerning the late Dr W. E. Sangster. When the famous Methodist preacher was a boy, he went away to a camp for a two-week holiday. During the middle of the first week he almost ran out of money. He sent a telegram to his father: 'S.O.S. Out of money. R.S.V.P.'

No answer came. The second week began and slipped away, and still no answer. His friends, noticing his preoccupation, said, 'Your Dad has forgotten you are here' and 'He is too busy to think about you.'

One of his friends asked him, 'What do you think?' He replied, 'I don't know what to think. It's all a mystery to me, but I'll wait until I get home, and he will tell me himself.'

When he got home it was all explained in one or two sentences. His father told him that, hard though it was for him not to respond, he saw this as one of the greatest opportunities he could have to learn the value

186

of money. Sangster said, 'I have known the value of money ever since.'

Some light shines out of the Scriptures on the dark problems of life, but no complete solution is given there. Every Christian must come to the place where he or she rests on this conviction: 'I'll wait until I get home, and he'll tell me himself.' The psalmist wrote, 'In righteousness I shall see your face; when I awake, I shall be satisfied with seeing your likeness' (Psalm 17:15).

This is the hour of triumph for God's people. A baptism of holy fire has come. Stunning, astounding signs, scenes, events are taking place throughout the world. You have read in these pages just some of the divine breakthroughs and victories that are being witnessed by the Holy Spirit's blessings. Jesus said 'Blessed is that servant, whom his Lord when he cometh shall find so doing' (Matthew 24:26). This entails acts of faith, renewed intercessions and challenging the works of darkness. Jesus is heaven's best. He is amongst us, we are moving in the glorious power of the Resurrection. Open the gates and the King of Glory will come in. In other words, expect a miracle . . . for 'We have received, not the spirit of the world, but the spirit which is of God, that we might freely know the things given to us of God' (1 Corinthians 2:12).

Due to the overwhelming response of thousands to the present awakening in the United Kingdom, through the commitment to God's guidance of the Rev. Melvin Banks, his family and their team, he personally or one of his family would be happy to make themselves available to visit your town, city, suburb, church or fellowship, in order to share these amazing stories and testimonies. Please contact the address given below.

The Rev. Melvin Banks welcomes letters, invitations, prayer requests for you or your loved ones.

Also available are videos, tapes and free literature. For the latest news of the Revival send a stamped addressed envelope to:

The Rev. Melvin Banks
International Crusade Office
44 Monks Way
Chippenham
Wiltshire
SN15 3TT
England
Tel: 01249 655712

If you would like further copies of this book, or other books by Melvin Banks – *Faith Unlimited, Is Anything Too Hard for God?, The Greatest Miracle, The Wind of Fire, With God All Things Are Possible* – please ask at your local Christian bookshop.